MARILYN MONROE

★ ★ ★ ★ ★ ★ ★ ★ ★ ★ ★ ★ ★ ★ ★ ★ ★ ★ ★

MARILYN
MONROE

★ ★ ★ ★ ★ ★ ★ ★ ★ ★ ★ ★ ★ ★ ★

FRANCES LEFKOWITZ

CHELSEA HOUSE PUBLISHERS

New York ★ Philadelphia

CHELSEA HOUSE PUBLISHERS

EDITORIAL DIRECTOR Richard Rennert
EXECUTIVE MANAGING EDITOR Karyn Gullen Browne
COPY CHIEF Robin James
PICTURE EDITOR Adrian G. Allen
CREATIVE DIRECTOR Robert Mitchell
ART DIRECTOR Joan Ferrigno
PRODUCTION MANAGER Sallye Scott

Pop Culture Legends
SENIOR EDITOR Kathy Kuhtz Campbell
SERIES DESIGN Basia Niemczyc

Staff for **MARILYN MONROE**
ASSISTANT EDITOR Joy Sanchez
EDITORIAL ASSISTANT Scott D. Briggs
PICTURE RESEARCHER Matthew Dudley
COVER ILLUSTRATION Alex Zwarenstein

3 5 7 9 8 6 4 2

Library of Congress Cataloging-in-Publication Data

Lefkowitz, Frances.
Marilyn Monroe/Frances Lefkowitz.
p. cm.—(Pop culture legends)
Includes bibliographical references and index.
ISBN 0-7910-2342-7
    0-7910-2367-2 (pbk.)
1. Monroe, Marilyn, 1926–1962—Juvenile literature. 2. Motion
picture actors and actresses—United States—Biography—Juvenile
literature. [1. Monroe, Marilyn, 1926–1962. 2. Actors and actresses. 3. Women—Biography.] I. Title. II. Series.
PN2287.M69L38 1995   94-36335
791.43'028'092—dc20   CIP
[B]   AC

FRONTISPIECE:
Marilyn Monroe poses over a subway grate in *The Seven
Year Itch.* This scene was filmed in New York City for
publicity purposes, but was completely reshot for the movie
in the Hollywood studio.

Contents ★

A Reflection of Ourselves

Leeza Gibbons

I ENJOY A RARE PERSPECTIVE on the entertainment industry. From my window on popular culture, I can see all that sizzles and excites. I have interviewed legends who have left us, such as Bette Davis and Sammy Davis, Jr., and have brushed shoulders with the names who have caused a commotion with their sheer outrageousness, like Boy George and Madonna. Whether it's by nature or by design, pop icons generate interest, and I think they are a mirror of who we are at any given time.

Who are *your* heroes and heroines, the people you most admire? Outside of your own family and friends, to whom do you look for inspiration and guidance, as examples of the type of person you would like to be as an adult? How do we decide who will be the most popular and influential members of our society?

You may be surprised by your answers. According to recent polls, you will probably respond much differently than your parents or grandparents did to the same questions at the same age. Increasingly, world leaders such as Winston Churchill, John F. Kennedy, Franklin D. Roosevelt, and evangelist Billy Graham have been replaced by entertainers, athletes, and popular artists as the individuals whom young people most respect and admire. In surveys taken during each of the past 15 years, for example, General Norman Schwarzkopf was the only world leader chosen as the number-one hero among high school students. Other names on the elite list joined by General Schwarzkopf included Paula Abdul, Michael Jackson, Michael Jordan, Eddie Murphy, Burt Reynolds, and Sylvester Stallone.

More than 30 years have passed since Canadian sociologist Marshall McLuhan first taught us the huge impact that the electronic media have had on how we think, learn, and understand—as well as how we choose our heroes. In the 1960s, Pop artist Andy Warhol predicted that there would soon come a time when every American would be famous for 15 minutes. But if it is easier today to achieve Warhol's 15 minutes of fame, it is also much harder to hold on to it. Reputations are often ruined as quickly as they are made.

And yet, there remain those artists and performers who continue to inspire and instruct us in spite of changes in world events, media technology, or popular tastes. Even in a society as fickle and fast moving as our own, there are still those performers whose work and reputation endure, pop culture legends who inspire an almost religious devotion from their fans.

Why do the works and personalities of some artists continue to fascinate us while others are so quickly forgotten? What, if any, qualities do they share that enable them to have such power over our lives? There are no easy answers to these questions. The artists and entertainers profiled in this series often have little more in common than the enormous influence that each of them has had on our lives.

Some offer us an escape. Artists such as actress Marilyn Monroe, comedian Groucho Marx, and writer Stephen King have used glamour, humor, or fantasy to help us escape from our everyday lives. Others present us with images that are all too recognizable. The uncompromising realism of actor and director Charlie Chaplin and folk singer Bob Dylan challenges us to confront and change the things in our world that most disturb us.

Some offer us friendly, reassuring experiences. The work of animator Walt Disney and late-night talk show host Johnny Carson, for example, provides us with a sense of security and continuity in a changing world. Others shake us up. The best work of composer John Lennon and actor James Dean will always inspire their fans to question and reevaluate the world in which they live.

It is also hard to predict the kind of life that a pop culture legend will lead, or how he or she will react to fame. Popular singers Michael Jackson

8

and Prince carefully guard their personal lives from public view. Other performers, such as popular singer Madonna, enjoy putting their private lives before the public eye.

What these artists and entertainers do share, however, is the rare ability to capture and hold the public's imagination in a world dominated by mass media and disposable celebrity. In spite of their differences, each of them has somehow managed to achieve legendary status in a popular culture that values novelty and change.

The books in this series examine the lives and careers of these and other pop culture legends, and the society that places such great value on their work. Each book considers the extraordinary talent, the stubborn commitment, and the great personal sacrifice required to create work of enduring quality and influence in today's world.

As you read these books, ask yourself the following questions: How are the careers of these individuals shaped by their society? What role do they play in shaping the world? And what is it that so captivates us about their lives, their work, or the images they present?

Hopefully, by studying the lives and achievements of these pop culture legends, we will learn more about ourselves.

★ Happy Birthday, Mr. President

TWENTY THOUSAND PEOPLE gathered at New York City's Madison Square Garden for a birthday party on Saturday, May 19, 1962. Millions more watched on television as entertainers from stage and screen sang, danced, and made jokes for the guest of honor. It was not just anybody's birthday: it was President John F. Kennedy's. He was turning 45 years old. And it was not just any party: it was a celebration of the triumph of the Democratic party and the popular young president it had helped elect. With movie stars and celebrities mingling with politicians and government officials, the festivity secured the glamorous image of the new presidency. And, with tickets for the event selling for $100 to $1,000, it was also an effective fund-raiser for the Democratic National Committee. All night long, comedian Jack Benny, the master of ceremonies, introduced performances by jazz vocalist Ella Fitzgerald, popular singers Peggy Lee and Harry Belafonte, and film actor Henry Fonda, among others. Now it was time to bring on the finale.

Marilyn Monroe, one of Hollywood's most popular entertainers, emanated seductive charm, poise, glamour, and humility, which endeared her forever to the public and the press.

★ MARILYN MONROE ★

Actor Peter Lawford, who was married to the president's sister Patricia Kennedy, had the honor of introducing the headlining act. Lawford, in fact, knew her personally. "Mr. President," he said from the podium, "on this occasion of your birthday, this lovely lady is not only pulchritudinous [beautiful] but punctual. . . ." There was a pause, but no one walked onstage. So Lawford continued. "A woman of whom it may truly be said 'she needs no introduction.' . . ." Still no one appeared. The headlining act, known for her chronic lateness, was nowhere to be found. The live audience, the television cameras, and the president of the United States all waited while Lawford continued to stall with an impromptu speech. "Mr. President, because, in the

On May 19, 1962, at President John F. Kennedy's 45th birthday gala, actor Peter Lawford presents Monroe to the attentive audience, saying that she is a woman who "needs no introduction."

history of show business, perhaps there has been no one female who has meant so much, who has done more. . . ." Finally she emerged from backstage, and at the sight of her, Lawford made one last joke with the audience. "Mr. President," he announced, "the *late* Marilyn Monroe."

The audience cheered as Marilyn Monroe, wrapped in ermine, walked slowly to the podium. The cheers continued as she slipped off the fur and revealed a stunning floor-length gown that glimmered and sparkled in the spotlights. Eventually the crowd hushed, and she began to sing. In what has become the most famous rendition of the world's most common song, Monroe sang "Happy Birthday" to the president. She infused the simple verse with the innocent sexiness that had made her famous. It was the same seductive charm that millions of fans had adored in musicals and comedies such as *Gentlemen Prefer Blondes* and *Some Like It Hot,* two of her most popular films. In her famous breathy voice, Monroe almost whispered the familiar tune to the president, who sat in a box seat in the balcony.

When she finished singing the four simple lines, she sang a few bars of a novelty song written especially for the occasion. To the tune of "Thanks for the Memories," the lyrics poked fun at the president and current political events. Then she led the audience in a reprise of "Happy Birthday." Seven minutes after taking the stage, amid deafening applause, she left, having changed the song and history forever.

The performance was pure Marilyn Monroe: enchanting yet effortless. And those who witnessed it had no idea of the complications and backstage trouble leading up to it. In the weeks prior to the birthday gala, composer Richard Adler, who was the prime organizer of the event, had heard stories about Monroe's preparation for the performance. Her dress was rumored to cost $12,000 and to be so formfitting that she would have to have it literally sewn around her the night of the show. Created by Hollywood designer Jean Louis, who had costumed Marlene Dietrich, it was made of flesh-colored sheer fabric and covered with beads and sequins, giving the illusion that Monroe was nude underneath the beads. Adler and several of the other gala organizers were worried that Monroe's costume and performance would be too racy, too inappropriate for a presidential salute. Up until the last moment, Adler, who had seen Monroe rehearse the number, was asking her to tone down her delivery and make it less sultry. He even considered asking her not to perform at the celebration.

But throughout her career, Monroe was adept at making the risqué acceptable and turning potential scandal into positive publicity. Part of her success came from her ability to gauge the likes and dislikes of the press and public. The audience's cheers at the gala showed Adler and the others that Monroe had once again endeared herself to the world. "It was like mass seduction," Adler said later, "with Marilyn whispering 'Happy Birthday' and the crowd yelling and screaming for her." When the president took the stage later, he too showed his appreciation. "Miss Monroe left a picture to come all the way East," he said, joking with the audience, "and I can now retire after having had 'Happy Birthday' sung to me in such a sweet, wholesome way."

But there had been other complications leading up to the performance. The motion picture that Kennedy referred to, *Something's Got To Give,* was in the middle of production and was plagued with problems. The film had become a disaster for Twentieth Century–Fox, the studio producing it. Early on, Monroe had secured permission from the studio to take a long weekend away from her work on the film in order to appear at the president's gala. But since that time, the filming had fallen behind sched-

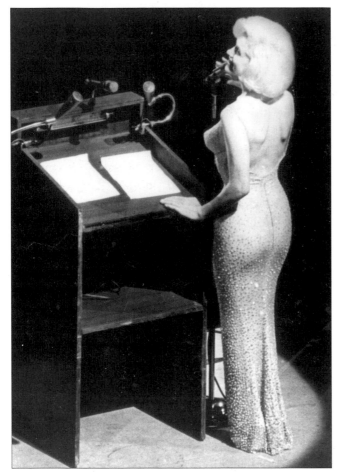

At the gala, wearing a beaded gown that was rumored to be literally sewn around her, Marilyn Monroe sings "Happy Birthday" to President Kennedy.

ule, and executives in charge of the production forbade Monroe to attend the celebration. Monroe believed, however, that the event was too important to miss. Despite their pleadings, she went ahead with her plans, and after finishing the filming of her scenes on May 17, she flew to New York. The next day, 24 hours before the celebration, Twentieth Century–Fox delivered a legal notice to her New York apartment. The letter stated that she was in breach of contract, and the implications were very clear: the studio was considering firing Marilyn Monroe.

It may seem unfathomable now that a film studio would fire its most famous star—one who had spent nearly her entire career on its roster and whose movies had earned the studio millions of dollars in revenue. But at the time, the movie business in general, and Twentieth Century–Fox in particular, were undergoing enormous financial, structural, and personnel changes. One faction of the new studio executives felt that Monroe was to blame for the problems with her latest film. Part of the problem, the studio claimed, was that Monroe had taken too many days off for being sick.

It was against this backdrop, of a gala committee that wanted to pull her from the show and a studio that wanted to fire her, that Monroe, who was nursing a viral cold, mounted the stage and sang "Happy Birthday" to the president. This performance, 10 days before President Kennedy's actual birthday, has gone on to become one of the most celebrated moments in the history of entertainment television, rivaling such moments as the appearances of Elvis Presley and the Beatles on the "Ed Sullivan Show." The footage has been replayed numerous times, and contemporary entertainers still parody it today. For Monroe, it was a perfect performance, drawing on everything she was famous for: her looks, her clothes, her walk, her breathy voice, her sultry singing, her earthy seductiveness, her provocative yet naive manner, and her ability to poke fun at her own glamorous image.

Part of the appeal of Marilyn Monroe was the aura of helplessness that surrounded her. It was not always clear how much of this aura emanated from the characters she played in the movies and how much came from her. Her childhood had been turbulent, with no father and a mother who was unable to care for her, and even after she grew up, she was rarely settled in one place for very long. But her beauty, charisma, and tenacity, teamed with years of hard work, enabled Monroe to work her way up the studio system to become one of its most famous stars. Eventually she would meet the queen of England, the premier of the Soviet Union, and the president of the United States, but she always made it seem like she was just a regular girl who happened to get lucky. "I feel as though it's all happening to someone right next to me," she said once about her enormous fame. "I'm close, I can feel it, I can hear it, but it isn't really me." Her charm and humility endeared her to the public and the press, which published countless interviews, articles, and photographs of her.

Monroe made the most of her popular appeal the night of the presidential gala. She had prepared fastidiously for her performance, rehearsing the song for weeks. In addition to the famous beaded gown, she also had a new hairstyle, which was flipped to the side and dyed an even whiter shade of blonde than usual. When she finally stepped onstage that evening, she was a powerful and captivating sight—an almost impossible combination of sexiness and wholesomeness, the consummation of qualities she had projected during her entire career.

At a private reception following the celebration, Monroe chatted with high-ranking politicians, including the president and his brother, Attorney General Robert Kennedy. White House adviser Arthur M. Schlesinger, Jr., who was at the reception, described Monroe as surrounded by "her own glittering mist." Although there were problems back home in California with her studio and her latest film and she was on medication for a severe cold, that night she seemed invincible.

Not three months later, on August 5, 1962, Marilyn Monroe died. She was discovered in her home in Los Angeles by her housekeeper. When the news of her death reached the public, it shocked the world. Her adoring fans could not believe that the vibrant, charismatic figure they idolized could be dead. There were countless ques-

President Kennedy (far right) watches a huge birthday cake as it is carried toward him at the Madison Square Garden gala in New York City. The event was also held to raise money for the Democratic party.

tions on the circumstances of her last weeks, and many people doubted the official cause of death, which authorities listed as "probable suicide" from an overdose of drugs. The deceased Marilyn Monroe seemed to take on another life, and the questions surrounding her death only added to her immortal status. During Monroe's life, her legend had consisted of vulnerability, purity, and sensuality. With her death, at age 36, it acquired another dimension: tragedy.

It did not take long for the rumors to spread. Theories on how and why she died, each one more outlandish than the last, have circulated for three decades. But the rumors were not just about her death. The press, which had propelled Monroe to immense fame while she was alive, now capitalized on that popularity. People who had had even the slightest contact with her, or who claimed to, came forth with their insights into the famous star. A host of men claimed to have had love affairs, even secret marriages with her. There were rumors of alcoholism and drug addiction, abortions, lost diaries, and illicit affairs with powerful figures. The biographies claiming to be the definitive portrait of the actress are numerous, and they continue to be published.

More than 30 years after her death, the public's fascination with Marilyn Monroe persists. Marilyn Monroe fan clubs still meet regularly, and she has a cult following that spans the globe. Monroe, or rather her legend, has also served as an inspiration to other artists, who have interpreted her and celebrated her in songs, plays, paintings, movies, and other works. Though the Monroe myth endures, much of it is based on hearsay, unsubstantiated rumors, and circumstantial evidence. Her performance at President Kennedy's birthday gala, for instance, has been used as part of an argument that Monroe and the president were involved in an affair. Similarly, almost every other event in her life is up for dispute. By now, the true story of her life and death has been so fictionalized that it is difficult to get through the myths, past the rumors, and down to the facts about the person called Marilyn Monroe.

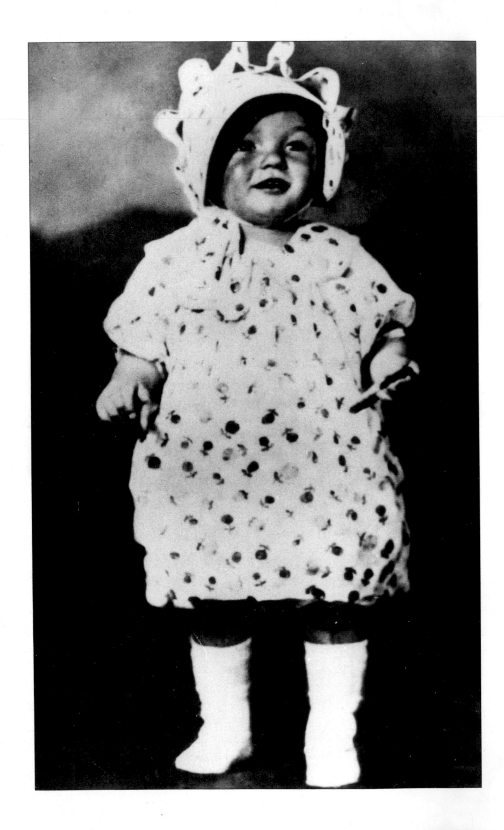

2 ★ Early Years: Norma Jeane

A T 9:30 IN THE MORNING on June 1, 1926, Gladys Monroe Baker Mortensen gave birth to a baby girl at California's Los Angeles General Hospital. Registering the child's birth, the 24-year-old Mortensen took a few liberties with the truth. She claimed that her two other children were dead, that her husband's name was Edward Mortenson, and that his whereabouts were unknown. In fact, her two children from her teenage marriage to John Newton Baker were alive and living with their father in Kentucky. Her current husband was named *Martin* Edward Mortensen, his last name spelled with two *es*. It may very well have been true, however, that she did not know his whereabouts, because they were separated and in the process of getting a divorce.

Gladys Mortensen named her daughter Norma Jeane. Settling on a last name was a bit more difficult, because Martin Mortensen had not fathered the baby. In fact, Gladys never revealed the identity of the father, who could have been one of several men that she had dated, including Charles Gifford, the man most often referred to as the father and a coworker at Consolidated Film Industries, where Gladys worked as a film splicer for motion pictures.

Norma Jeane Mortensen, later known as Marilyn Monroe, never knew the identity of her father. Some say that her mother only told her that her father looked like the screen idol Clark Gable.

But Norma Jeane, who sometimes went by the last name Baker, after her mother's first husband, and at other times by the name of Mortensen, after her mother's second husband, never knew who her father was. One long-standing story is that Norma Jeane's mother told her that her father looked like Clark Gable, and forever after she imagined that the screen idol was actually her father.

Almost immediately after giving birth, Gladys Mortensen brought Norma Jeane to live with a foster family, headed by Ida and Albert Bolender, who raised the little girl until she was seven years old. It is not entirely clear why Mortensen decided to have someone else rear her daughter, although certainly the pressures of being a single working mother in the 1920s and 1930s were immense. The Great Depression made times hard and money scarce, there were no child-care centers, and Mortensen needed to work full-time. Mortensen might simply not have had the interest or commitment necessary for raising a child. She had virtually no contact with her other two children. In addition, Mortensen's mother, Della Hogan Monroe, who also lived in the Los Angeles area, seemed to agree that sending the child to live with the Bolenders was the best idea.

Ida and Albert Bolender were strict, religious, and competent caretakers who had in their charge several other children besides Norma Jeane. Mortensen paid them $25 each month to care for Norma Jeane. Though Mortensen kept in touch with the Bolenders and visited her daughter occasionally, Norma Jeane grew up without a consistent and intimate parental figure in her life. Her mother's visits often confused her, and Norma Jeane thought of Mortensen not as her mother but as "the woman with the red hair." As she recounted later, "One morning I called [Ida] 'Mother' and she said 'Don't call me that—I'm not your mother. Call me "Aunt Ida." Then I pointed to her husband, and I said 'But he's my

Daddy!' and she just said 'No.'" Although not overly warm or sentimental, the Bolenders were caring and dedicated foster parents who stressed morality and good manners in their household.

In 1933, just after Norma Jeane's seventh birthday, her mother decided to take her back from the foster family. One version of this episode claims that the Bolenders asked Mortensen to visit because Norma Jeane was upset over the death of her pet dog, Tippy. For whatever reason, after her visit Mortensen decided that Norma Jeane should come live with her. Mother and daughter lived for two months in an apartment in Hollywood and then moved into a three-bedroom house that Mortensen purchased. To help with expenses, they shared their house with another family, the Atkinsons, who worked in Hollywood as movie extras and stand-ins. In addition,

Norma Jeane as a toddler poses on the running board of a Model A Ford. She lived with various foster families, relatives, friends, and even in an orphanage as a child, because her mother was unable to care for her.

Mortensen's best friend from the film lab, Grace McKee, often visited. Norma Jeane's new home could not have been more different from the stoic, sturdy home where she had grown up. Her new extended family did not follow the same rules as the Bolenders had—this house was rowdy and boisterous, filled with card playing, drinking, and dancing.

But the changes had just begun. Less than a year later, Mortensen suffered from a bout of depression and began to withdraw from the people around her. Finally she became so incapable of coping with her life that she

Norma Jeane is shown here as a four-year-old with her arm around a playmate. She grew up without a constant and affectionate parental figure in her life.

entered a rest home, and then a hospital. In the 1930s, the medical establishment did not understand or treat psychological disorders very well, and thus the nature of Mortensen's affliction has never been known for certain. If she had today's array of therapeutic services and medications available to her, she might have fared better. As it was, she spent most of the remainder of her life in a variety of rest homes, hospitals, and sanatoriums and lost all chances of being a mother to Norma Jeane.

For Norma Jeane, the rest of childhood was filled with chaos and instability as she moved among foster families, relatives, family friends, and even an orphanage. At first she lived in her mother's home with the Atkinsons, with frequent visits from her mother's friend Grace McKee. In 1935, Mortensen was declared legally insane, and McKee applied to become Norma Jeane's legal guardian. With nowhere to go, Norma Jeane spent ages 9 through 11 at the Los Angeles Orphans Home. In 1937, McKee, who had since married Ervin "Doc" Goddard, became her guardian and took Norma Jeane into her home.

But the uncertainty of her living situations continued. After just six months with "Aunt Grace" and her family, Norma Jeane was shipped off to live with some distant relatives in Compton, on the other side of Los Angeles County. There is some speculation that Doc Goddard may have attempted to molest Norma Jeane and that this incident was the reason she was sent away. As an adult, Norma Jeane recalled that this time in her life was very confusing: "At first I was waking up in the mornings at the Goddards' and thinking I was still at the orphanage. Then, before I could get used to them I was with another aunt and uncle, waking up and thinking I was still at the Goddards."

Less than a year later, the 12-year-old returned to Los Angeles, this time to live with Grace Goddard's aunt, 58-year-old Ana Lower. Of all the parental figures

Norma Jeane had, "Aunt Ana" was the one to whom she felt the closest. As she said later, Lower "was the first person in the world I ever really loved. . . . She was the only one who loved and understood me." Lower was devoted to the Christian Science religion, and she and Norma Jeane attended the services of the Church of Christ, Scientist, regularly.

While living with Lower, Norma Jeane entered Emerson Junior High School in West Los Angeles, where she was a shy, average student, with a slight stammer in her speech. She was not very popular, though she grew more gregarious by the time she graduated in 1941. In her last year she wrote for the school newspaper, the *Emersonian*. But she never overcame her anxiety and nervousness

Norma Jeane was an average student at Emerson Junior High School in West Los Angeles, where she was considered by classmates to be a shy girl with few friends. It was not until her last year there, when she started to mature and wear makeup, that the boys noticed her and the girls wanted to be her friend. A classmate later said, "Suddenly she just seemed to stand out in a crowd."

about speaking in public, as evidenced by poor grades in her rhetoric (public speaking) classes.

In her final semester of junior high school, Norma Jeane had to move back to the Goddards' house in Van Nuys because Lower had developed health problems. She now gained a sister of sorts: Eleanor "Bebe" Goddard, the daughter of Doc Goddard from a previous marriage, who had just come to live with her father and Grace. Bebe had also had a troubled and chaotic childhood, and she and Norma Jeane, who were about the same age, got along well. In the fall they enrolled together at Van Nuys High School. Though still an average student, Norma Jeane was more outgoing and social than she had been in junior high school. But soon the Goddards got word that Doc was being transferred by his employer, and the family would be moving to West Virginia. They elected not to take Norma Jeane with them, and she moved, in the middle of her first year of high school, back with Ana Lower, whose health had improved. She enrolled at University High School to begin her second semester of the 10th grade. As it turned out, she did not finish the year.

Since the fall of 1941, Norma Jeane had been friendly with a neighbor of the Goddards', Jim Dougherty, who was five years older than she. Having already graduated from high school, Dougherty worked at Lockheed Aircraft, a manufacturer of defense equipment. They began to date, and in mid-March Norma Jeane quit school, announcing that she would marry Dougherty in June, as soon as she turned 16 (the legal age for marriage in California). It appears that Grace Goddard might have had a lot to do with arranging this marriage. Not wanting to take Norma Jeane along with her family to West Virginia, she needed to find a home for her. How much she hinted or suggested marriage to Jim and his mother, and how much Norma Jeane was aware of these sugges-

On June 19, 1942, Norma Jeane married her neighbor, Jim Dougherty, when she was 16 and he was 21. Although she later claimed that it was a union of convenience, Norma Jeane wrote one year after their marriage, "I love him so very much, honestly, I don't think there is another man alive like him."

tions, is not known for certain. It is conceivable that Jim and Norma Jeane would not have married so quickly, or perhaps at all, had Norma Jeane not been abandoned by the Goddards. Years later she would claim that they had gotten married so she would not have to go back to the orphanage. But at the time, Jim and Norma Jeane enjoyed each other's company. In his words, "Our marriage may have been made in some place short of heaven, like in the minds of two older ladies, but there was no pretense in how Norma Jeane and I felt about each other once we'd formed that partnership." When they were married on June 19, 1942, they approached their life together with both pragmatism and optimism.

Norma Jeane spent the first year of her marriage as a housewife, while Jim went to work each day at Lockheed. In Europe and Asia the battles of World War II were raging, and the United States was supplying munitions as well as armed forces to the Allied cause. Soon Jim joined the Merchant Marine, and he and Norma Jeane went to live on nearby Catalina Island, where he was stationed. Although there was a scarcity of women for Norma Jeane to befriend, the couple was social, making friends and going to parties and dances. In the spring of 1944, however, Jim was sent overseas, and Norma Jeane went to live with his mother in North Hollywood.

During World War II, women in the United States entered the work force in unprecedented numbers. The war, which boosted the American economy, created a huge demand for defense supplies and equipment, much of which was manufactured in U.S. factories. With so many young men enlisted in the armed services, it was left to the women to fill vital jobs at home. Soon Norma Jeane, with the help of her mother-in-law, was to become one of the millions of "Rosie the Riveters," the women who worked in industrial positions during the war, fastening steel rivets, among other traditionally male jobs. Ethel Dougherty, who worked as a nurse at an aircraft manufacturer called the Radioplane Company, helped Norma Jeane find a job there as well. Norma Jeane's assignments included spraying glue on aircraft fabric (in what was called the "dope room") and inspecting and folding parachutes. At $20 a week, she was earning the nation's minimum wage at the time.

After a childhood of chaos and instability, Norma Jeane Dougherty finally seemed settled in a secure and comfortable life. She worked 60 hours a week, visited Aunt Ana, and wrote letters to her husband overseas. Though the marriage may have been based on necessity, she had grown attached to Jim Dougherty. As she explained in a letter to her former guardian Grace McKee Goddard in December 1941, "I love him so very much, honestly, I don't think there is another man alive like him."

3 Discovery

IN THE MYTHOLOGY OF HOLLYWOOD movie stars, there is always the moment when a star is discovered. Marilyn Monroe, whose life story over the years has been twisted and turned to fit in with this mythology, has come to embody the cliché of a shy nobody who gets discovered and sent on the road to fame and fortune. During her lifetime, and after her death as well, many people claimed to be the first to notice her star potential. These "discoverers," with the benefit of hindsight, maintained that there was an almost clairvoyant moment when they saw the incredible success that awaited Norma Jeane. They imply that in a single moment they unearthed her talent and foresaw her great future, and from then on she was just following the path of destiny.

The truth is, there were many moments in Monroe's life, and numerous people and events that affected her future and swayed the direction that her life and career took. But none of these influences would have had any impact had she not possessed talent, interest, ambition, and the ability to channel these traits into her work.

While working at an airplane factory in late 1944, Norma Jeane was discovered by a U.S. Army photographer who was taking pictures of women working for the war effort. The photographer encouraged Norma Jeane to quit her job and try modeling.

Late in 1944, Norma Jeane Dougherty, as she was still known, was working at the Radioplane Company when a crew of U.S. Army photographers visited the factory. As part of a publicity campaign to drum up support for the American war effort and elevate the morale of the soldiers, the U.S. Army had established the First Motion Picture Unit. The photographers came to Radioplane to take publicity pictures of women working at the factory. Norma Jeane described the occasion soon afterward in a letter to Grace McKee Goddard:

> The first thing I knew they had me out there, taking pictures of me. . . . They all asked where in the H— I had been hiding. . . . They took a lot of moving pictures of me, and some of them asked for dates, etc. (*Naturally I refused!*) . . . After they finished with some of the pictures, an army colonel by the name of David Conover told me he would be interested in getting some color still shots of me.

Conover was one of the people who later claimed to have discovered the young woman who was to become Marilyn Monroe. In 1981, almost 40 years after his encounter with Norma Jeane, he wrote a book entitled *Finding Marilyn,* with the subtitle *A Romance by David Conover, the Man Who Discovered Marilyn Monroe.* In the book he describes his first view of Norma Jeane, at the assembly line, with "curly ash blonde hair and her face . . . smudged with dirt." He remembers her as timid but "her response to the camera then was amazing . . . she came alive with sure and immediate instinct."

In his book, Conover claims he saw "something special about her, a luminous quality to her face, a fragileness with astonishing vibrancy. This girl was going places. I could feel it in my bones." Conover also asserts that he told the young Norma Jeane, "Someday you're going to be a famous movie star." His description of the woman who would later become a legend is similar to the descriptions of many other people who claim to have discovered her. But whether or not Conover had the foresight to predict Norma Jeane's future, he certainly played a key role in introducing her to a career in modeling. After several photo sessions, Conover advised her to quit factory work and try modeling full-time.

On August 2, 1945, Norma Jeane applied for entrance at the Blue Book Model Agency. At Blue Book, Monroe took a variety of classes in grooming and modeling and had her light brown hair dyed to a golden shade of blonde. She was at work almost immediately on a variety of assignments, including modeling clothes and posing for photographs to be used in advertisements and on magazine covers.

Modeling was certainly more lucrative and more enjoyable than the work she had done at the factory, and she approached her new career with excitement. Her enthusiasm, her photogenic qualities, and her reputation for being pleasant to work with helped move her career forward at a fast pace. In less than a year, she appeared on the covers of 33 popular magazines, including *Laff, Peek,* and *Parade.* However, she was not without misgivings about this new profession that focused so much attention on her appearance. As she said later, "You smile for the camera, you hold very still, you act as if you are having a good time. . . . I guess I shouldn't say this, but sometimes modeling just seemed so phoney and fake."

All the changes that came with embarking on a new career soon affected other aspects of Norma Jeane's life. Her marriage to Jim Dougherty, who was stationed overseas most of the time, was no longer satisfactory. When they first got married, Norma Jeane had few outside interests or friends, and she waited with anticipation for Jim's homecomings. Now she had an exciting new profession, which her husband, whose view of marriage was "I'm the captain and my wife is first mate," did not relish. Years later, Norma Jeane would say that the

marriage "brought me neither happiness nor pain. My husband and I hardly spoke to each other. This wasn't because we were angry. We had nothing to say." Jim Dougherty would later refute this depiction, saying, "I wonder if she's forgotten how much in love we really were."

In the summer of 1946, Norma Jeane went to Las Vegas, Nevada, where divorces (and marriages) are easily and quickly obtained, and filed for divorce. Through her lawyer, she sent a letter to her husband overseas, informing him of her plans. In Nevada, she stayed with a relative of her former guardian Grace McKee Goddard, and on September 13 the state granted her a divorce.

That same year Norma Jeane took the first steps toward breaking into the movies. This desire may have been a factor in her decision to divorce Dougherty. Some biographers have suggested that several people, including Emmeline Snively of the Blue Book Agency, advised Norma Jeane that a married woman would have trouble making it in the movie industry. According to biographer Donald Spoto, Snively, among others, told Norma Jeane about the constraints of studio life. The studios were reluctant to hire married women for fear that they would get pregnant and quit and that being married jarred with the image of a young, available starlet. In any case, Norma Jeane signed up with a talent agency, National Concert Artists Corporation, and soon had a meeting with Ben Lyon, an executive at Twentieth Century–Fox, one of Hollywood's premier film studios. Lyon arranged for Norma Jeane to make a screen test, which is a short film done to see how a person's looks, presence, and acting ability translate to the screen. On July 19, 1946, she reported to a movie set on the studio's Hollywood lot, along with director Walter Lang, cinematographer Leon Shamroy, makeup artist Allan "Whitey" Snyder, and other studio technicians who filmed the short test. Shot

OPPOSITE:
When Norma Jeane joined the Blue Book Model Agency in August 1945, she took classes in modeling, makeup, and grooming and posed frequently for photographer Joseph Jasgur, who took this picture. By the following spring, she had appeared on the covers of 33 magazines, and according to Blue Book owner Emmeline Snively, "[Norma Jeane] wanted to learn, wanted to be somebody, more than anybody I ever saw before in my life."

in Technicolor without sound, Norma Jeane followed instructions and completed a few simple actions—walking, sitting on a stool, and lighting a cigarette—to demonstrate how she appeared on film.

According to Shamroy, Norma Jean's brief performance that day gave him "a cold chill." "This girl had something I hadn't seen since silent pictures. She had a kind of fantastic beauty like Gloria Swanson . . . and she got sex on a piece of film like Jean Harlow." Speaking five years after the occasion, Shamroy claimed that he recognized her great future immediately, and offered this insight: "Her natural beauty plus her inferiority complex gave her a look of mystery."

Ben Lyon was impressed enough with her performance in the test to secure permission from Darryl F. Zanuck, the studio's vice-president in charge of production, to sign her up. In August 1946, she signed a six-month contract, standard for a fledgling starlet, and joined the ranks of thousands of other contract players who worked for the movie studios.

Under the Hollywood studio system, which was in effect from just before 1930 to the late 1940s, eight corporations produced more than 90 percent of American movies. Of these corporations, the "Big Five"—Metro-Goldwyn-Mayer

(MGM), Paramount, Radio-Keith-Orpheum (RKO), Twentieth Century–Fox, and Warner Bros.—owned the production facilities (the studios) and many of the exhibition venues (the theaters). Controlling both the production end and the exhibition end, as well as the means of distribution between these two, allowed the Big Five to earn huge profits. These earnings, in turn, gave the studio executives enormous power over anyone who wanted to make a living in the movies.

Norma Jeane was extremely excited about her new career as a model, but her husband was not as enthusiastic. While Dougherty was overseas serving with the merchant marine, he felt that her "hobby" was fine, but told her, "When I get out of the service we're going to have a family and you're going to settle down." Their marriage ended shortly thereafter.

The studio system has often been compared with the slave system, with the actors, writers, directors, and other contracted employees perceived as chattel and the production chiefs viewed as bosses. Another way to look at the system is as a highly efficient factory that consolidated all of the equipment, from cameras to costumes, and the personnel, from actors to electricians, necessary to make a movie. Contracted employees, including directors, writers, and makeup artists, showed up at the studio, got their assignments, and went to work. This centralized system allowed the studios to churn out movies at an incredible rate—more than 500 in 1937, compared to about 250 in the 1950s and less than 100 made in the United States in 1978. Although the quality of the movies varied, their sheer quantity and popularity established the studio era of the 1930s and 1940s as Hollywood's Golden Age.

Part of the efficiency of the studio system derived from the control that the studio bosses maintained over the public and private lives of their actors. To work in the movies, actors had to sign contracts stipulating that they would accept any role in any movie assigned to them and that they would participate in all publicity assignments, including photographs, public appearances, and interviews. Furthermore, under the "morals clause," the studio regulated the actor's public behavior. The executives chose a public image for the actors and could require them to dress a certain way, to date a particular person, or even to have facial surgery to fit that image. The penalty for breaking any clause in the contract or not complying with directions was suspension without pay. And while the actor was under contract, he or she could not work elsewhere, not even as a dishwasher in a restaurant. Some actors who became successful stars eventually battled the studio powers for autonomy over their careers and personal lives. But for most of them, the studio era

OPPOSITE:
Norma Jeane made the transformation from model to actress when she signed a six-month contract with Twentieth Century–Fox in August 1946. Most of the work she did for the studio during this time was publicity-related—posing for photographs, giving interviews, and making public appearances. It was also in 1946 that a studio executive changed Norma Jeane's name to Marilyn Monroe.

was a time when not complying with the bosses could mean suspension, blacklisting, and sometimes even the end of a career.

In August 1946, when Norma Jeane Dougherty became the latest young hopeful to join the legion of contract players at Twentieth Century–Fox, the studio system was beginning to weaken under changing economic conditions, and the movie industry was in a state of transition. Nonetheless, her contract, which paid her $75 per week for six months, was similar to the contracts signed by struggling actors during the heyday of the studio system. At age 20 she was still a minor, and so her legal guardian, Grace McKee Goddard, had to cosign the contract. Once the contract was signed, there was one more matter to take care of: choosing a screen name for Norma Jeane.

There are many stories about the changing of Norma Jeane Dougherty's name to Marilyn Monroe. Some versions claim Ben Lyon called Norma Jeane into his office at the studio and told her that her name was too cumbersome. Another version maintains that Norma Jeane visited Lyon and his wife at their beach house to discuss possibilities for her new screen name. Most agree that Lyon suggested the first name, Marilyn, because of its reference to renowned theater actress Marilyn Miller, who had died in 1936. The last name, Monroe, was Norma Jeane's family name, the maiden name of her mother. It has also been suggested that the two *M*s were chosen because Norma Jeane, who stammered slightly when nervous, had been known in high school as "The Mmmmm Girl."

It is not clear when exactly Norma Jeane began to think about becoming a movie star. Some biographers believe it was a wish she had had since childhood; others have suggested that Grace McKee Goddard fostered Norma Jeane's movie dreams by constantly comparing her to actress Jean Harlow. There is also the possibility that she had never thought about a career in films until her modeling agent mentioned it to her. What is clear is that once Norma Jeane decided on her profession, she worked with dedication and diligence to achieve success.

4 ★ The Starlet

ALTHOUGH SHE WAS SIGNED UP with a major film studio, it took a while for Norma Jeane, now known as Marilyn Monroe, to appear in a film. For the first six months of her contract, her assignments were mostly publicity-related—she appeared in photographs and at live events promoting the studio. Like many aspiring studio actresses, Monroe had no dramatic training and almost no acting experience, and had been signed mostly for her looks. The experience she had as a model, however, came in handy. Newspapers and magazines made constant requests to the studio publicity departments for news and photographs of the starlets, and Monroe posed for many of these pictures. The news items that the publicists included with the photographs were usually fabricated stories of the starlet's discovery and her personal history—stories that had very little to do with the facts. One of Monroe's early appearances in the media, for example, was in the *Los Angeles Times* in January 1947. A photo of her in a two-piece bathing suit ran under the headline, "Baby Sitter Lands in Films." The caption said that the "18-

Joseph Schenck, one of the founders of Twentieth Century–Fox, greatly influenced Marilyn Monroe's career; he introduced her to the head of Columbia Pictures, who offered her a six-month contract and her first major role in a movie. Monroe is seen here with Schenck in 1959, about 10 years after they first met.

year-old blonde baby sitter walked into a studio talent scout's home." Monroe, who was 20 years old, had done no such thing.

Aside from her publicity work, Monroe had no assignments and a lot of free time. Eager to learn the movie business, she would report to the studio lot to visit the different departments and ask questions about lighting, wardrobe, makeup, publicity, and all the other aspects of the movie business. Monroe was "desperate to absorb all she could," according to Whitey Snyder, one of the chief makeup artists at the studio. Columnist Sidney Skolsky also remarked on her determination: "It was clear that Marilyn was prepared to work hard to improve herself." About this determination, Monroe would later say, "My illusions didn't have anything to do with being a fine actress. I knew how third rate I was. I could actually feel my lack of talent, as if it were cheap clothes I was wearing inside. But, my God, how I wanted to learn! To change, to improve!"

Six months later her contract was renewed, and she was cast in her first movie. Given a very small role— hardly more than an extra in a minor picture—Monroe played in two scenes as a teenager in *Scudda-Hoo! Scudda-Hay!*, a light romance that takes place in the countryside. She appears in one scene in a rowboat on a lake, and in the other she walks by one of the central characters. The scenes are so brief and Monroe is at such a distance that it would take a great deal of attention to notice her in the film. Her one speaking line, "Hi, Rad," delivered to the lead character, happens so quickly that it can barely be heard. It was not exactly an auspicious debut; she did not even receive a credit in the film. But a few months later, in May, she was cast in a slightly larger role in a somewhat better film called *Dangerous Years*.

Another story about teenagers, *Dangerous Years* was a B picture (a small-budget movie) about a hoodlum and the group of juvenile delinquents who come under his influence in a small town. Monroe plays Eve, a sassy waitress at The Gopher Hole, the neighborhood restaurant where the teenagers hang out and play the jukebox. With three scenes and several speaking lines, Monroe was listed in the credits of this film, which is considered her first real movie role. It was released in December 1947, four months before *Scudda-Hoo! Scudda-Hay!* was shown in theaters.

Aside from these two minor film roles and the spate of publicity assignments, Monroe spent her first year as a contract player learning how to act. Twentieth Century–Fox paid for Monroe and other contract players to attend classes at the Actors Laboratory. Led by Phoebe Brand and Morris Carnovsky, two theater actors who had been trained at the prominent Group Theater in New York, the Laboratory was a place for actors, directors, and playwrights to develop and present plays on the West Coast. Like the Group Theater, the Actors Laboratory cultivated serious plays about serious themes dealing with the depression, the labor movement, and other social issues in the country. Such acclaimed theater figures as playwrights Tennessee Williams and Clifford Odets and actor-director Elia Kazan spent time at the Actors Laboratory honing their craft. As Monroe said later, the Actors Laboratory "was as far from *Scudda Hoo! Scudda Hay!* as you could get. It was my first taste of what real acting in real drama could be, and I was hooked."

It was not just the subject matter of the plays that differed from the movies produced at the studio. It was also the environment and the working methods. At the studio, where Monroe had been hired on the basis of her appearance, the movies emphasized beauty and entertainment, and the plot lines stayed mostly on the surface, avoiding controversy in their attempt to appeal to as many people as possible. Money, reflected in box office success, dictated the type and nature of films that were made. At the Actors Laboratory the emphasis was on the art and craft of dramas that dealt with complex issues of modern life. There Monroe read and studied plays, watched productions, and participated in acting exercises. She said later,

> All I could think of was this far, far away place called New York, where actors and directors did very different things than stand around all day arguing about a close up or a camera angle. I had never seen a play and I don't think I knew how to read one very well. But Phoebe Brand and her company somehow made it all very real. It seemed so exciting to me, and I wanted to be a part of that life.

But when her contract came to term in August 1947, the executives at Twentieth Century–Fox decided not to renew it. Monroe continued to take classes at the Actors Laboratory at her own expense, but without a job, she would soon have to give up her studies there. It is often said about the entertainment industry that "it's who you know" that gets a person ahead, and that meeting the right people can make or break a career. It is true that it takes more than talent to be a success, but it would be more accurate to say that for someone with talent and aspirations, the future hinges on meeting people who recognize her or his potential and who are in a position to make

Determined to become a star, Monroe did everything possible to develop into a well-rounded actress. She seriously studied plays and took lessons in acting, voice, and dance.

something of it. At this point in her life, Monroe had either the good fortune, the good sense, or both, to befriend several people who recognized her talent and helped call attention to it.

The first of these important acquaintances was the Hollywood couple Lucille Ryman and John Carroll. Ryman, who ran the talent department at the MGM studios, and her husband, Carroll, who was a film actor, met Monroe at a celebrity golf tournament. Just before her contract expired at Fox, Monroe and other starlets were sent to the tournament to serve as caddies for the stars. The couple befriended Monroe, and upon hearing that she had just lost her job at the studio, Ryman and Carroll offered to help her financially. As experienced professionals in the movie business, they knew how hard it was for a young hopeful who was just starting out. They soon became Monroe's informal sponsors, because she seemed to have no friends or family. And early that fall, Monroe moved in with Ryman and Carroll, who had two homes, so she would not have to pay rent while she searched for film roles. She continued with her acting classes and also appeared in a three-week run of a student stage play, the comedy *Glamour Preferred*.

Several months later, at a party in early 1948, Monroe met a second pivotal person in her career: Joseph Schenck. Schenck, who was almost 70 years old, was one of the founders of Twentieth Century–Fox. Some have referred to Monroe during this time as "Joe Schenck's girl," and the exact nature of their relationship is not clear. Schenck, who was at that time an executive producer at Twentieth Century–Fox, did not use his influence to re-sign Monroe to the studio. He did, however, arrange for her to meet with his friend Harry Cohn, who was the head of Columbia Pictures. Through this meeting, Monroe signed another six-month contract, at the rate of $125 per week.

Though brief, Monroe's stay at Columbia had a lasting impact on her career. Almost immediately the studio executives, who had the authority to determine an image for their contract players, decided that Monroe should be a blonde. They changed her hair color from its brownish dirty blonde to a whiter, golden shade. Columbia then assigned Monroe an acting coach. Natasha Lytess, the head drama coach at the studio, began working with Monroe in the spring of 1948, teaching her acting, voice, and diction. Monroe was instantly impressed with Lytess, who had emigrated from Europe and was well educated in the history of acting and the theater. "She was like a waterfall, pouring out impressions and images," said Monroe. "I just sat there watching her expressive hands and flashing eyes, and listening to her confident voice speak about the Russian soul. She told me what she had been through and made it clear how much she knew. But she gave me the impression that I was something special, too."

The relationship became intense very early on, with Monroe anxious to learn all that she could, and Lytess eager to teach her. With this intensity came complications. As Monroe later said, "There were days when I couldn't figure out why she kept me on as a student, because she made me feel so shallow and without talent." Nonetheless, Monroe, who did not live in one place for very long, moved in with her teacher for a short time. Lytess later claimed to have recognized, and even developed, Monroe's talent in these early stages of Monroe's career, asserting that "I taught her how to walk, how to breathe."

One facet of her student's career that definitely concerned Lytess was the studio's tendency to typecast Monroe as a dumb, sexy blonde. At the same time that the studio executives were dyeing her hair and focusing on her appearance, the studio acting coach was stressing

OPPOSITE:
Columbia Pictures assigned Monroe an acting coach, Natasha Lytess (left), with whom she worked from 1948 to 1953. While the studio was typecasting Monroe as a dumb blonde, Lytess was teaching her the art of serious acting.

the art and craft of dramatic performance. This conflict between her image and her deeper artistic desires would continue throughout Monroe's life. As Lytess said later, "There's more to Marilyn than meets the eye. The trouble is that when people look at her they immediately figure her as a typical Hollywood blonde. It's not their fault though. Marilyn's soul just doesn't fit her body."

In any case, Monroe's diligent training soon paid off, and she was cast in a major role in a minor musical at Columbia called *Ladies of the Chorus.* Playing Peggy, a stage dancer who marries a society man, Monroe had her largest role yet, one that included singing two songs. Her preparations for the role included singing lessons with the studio's vocal coach and music arranger, Fred Karger. All her hard work on the movie was worthwhile: in the fall of 1948, Monroe was mentioned in her first review. The article in the trade magazine *Motion Picture Herald* stated, "One of the bright spots is Monroe's singing. She is pretty and, with her pleasing voice and style, she shows promise."

By now, Monroe was living in her own apartment at the Studio Club, a relatively inexpensive residential hotel in Hollywood that housed young women desiring a career in the movie industry. She still kept in close contact with Lucille Ryman and John Carroll and continued to receive money from them. For the most part, she had cut herself off from the people she knew when she was growing up. She had little contact with her mother, who remained institutionalized, or with Grace McKee Goddard, who was living out of state. With the death of Ana Lower in March 1948, Monroe had nearly no family or friends from her past. Almost everyone she knew she had met through her work. She soon became friends with Fred Karger, the vocal coach at Columbia, who was well established in Hollywood and gave Monroe advice on how to make it there. He also introduced her to his family—his mother, his sister, and his daughter from an earlier marriage—who welcomed Monroe into their home. Karger was important to Monroe, but the romantic aspect of their relationship was rocky. Monroe knew that "he liked me and was happy to be with me but his love didn't seem anything like mine. Most of his talk to me was a form of criticism. He kept pointing out how little I knew and how unaware of life I was." However, the warmth of his family, with whom she lived briefly, was significant, as was the work that Karger and Monroe accomplished on her singing.

Shortly after the release of *Ladies of the Chorus,* Monroe's contract came up for renewal at Columbia. The studio declined to renew it, and Monroe was out of a job. With her allowance from Ryman and Carroll, she continued lessons with Lytess. And soon Monroe made another contact with someone who recognized her talent and had the power to make something of it. At a party in late 1948, Monroe met Johnny Hyde, executive vice-president of the powerful William Morris talent agency. Hyde, who was married and under a doctor's care for cardiopulmonary problems, represented such movie stars as Rita Hayworth, Lana Turner, and Bob Hope. In the mythology of the stardom of Marilyn Monroe, it is Hyde who is generally given the most credit for having discovered her. The story is told that he immediately fell in love with Monroe and took her career in his hands. Hyde told Monroe she was going to be a star and then used all his influence to help make it happen. "Yes, it's there. I can feel it. I see a hundred actresses a week. They haven't got what you have," he told her. Officially, he became her agent, as he bought her contract out from her agent at National Concert Artists. Unofficially, he became her friend, lover, adviser, and mentor.

Though the relationship between the 22-year-old aspiring starlet and the 53-year-old agent might have looked suspicious, by most accounts the personal feelings between them were genuine. Hyde, who left his family, wanted Monroe to marry him and live with him in his newly rented home in Beverly Hills. But despite deep feelings for Hyde, Monroe was not in love with him and refused his proposal. Monroe knew what their relationship looked like to other people, and knew it would look even worse if she married Hyde. "Johnny Hyde gave me more than his kindness and love. He was the first man I had ever known who understood me. Most men (and women) thought I was scheming and two-faced. No matter how truthfully I spoke to them or how honestly I behaved, they always believed I was trying to fool them." Though they were frequently together, she maintained her own residence at the Beverly Carlton Hotel.

The first audition Monroe's new agent arranged for her was for a small role in a Marx Brothers comedy called *Love Happy*, filmed in 1949 and released in 1950. The plot was typical of the zany Marx Brothers movies and involved a detective, a diamond smuggler, and a can of sardines. Monroe was cast in the role of a gorgeous young woman who tries to enlist the help of the detective, played by Groucho Marx. Her brief scene called for her to wear a tight, revealing dress and to tell the detective that she needs his help because "Some men are following me." She then walks across the room as Groucho, and the camera, stare at her rear. Groucho raises his eyebrows and says in his most sarcastic voice, "Really? I can't understand why."

It was a one-joke role, and Monroe played it with a balance of exaggerated sexiness and naïveté. Groucho's assessment of Monroe was that "She's Mae West, Theda Bara and Bo Peep all rolled into one." And though the role was small—it lasted about a minute on-screen—it was Monroe's most visible performance yet. She became an integral part of the movie's publicity campaign and

was sent to Chicago, New York, and other cities to talk to reporters, have her picture taken, and promote interest in the movie.

Monroe spent most of 1949 and 1950 diligently training and auditioning. Though she was not offered a studio contract, she did get cast in several films on a per-picture basis. The first of these was a minor musical Western called *A Ticket to Tomahawk* for Twentieth Century–Fox, which she did immediately after her promotional tour for *Love Happy*. She had a small role as a chorus girl.

Her next part, though small, was very important for Monroe. Many consider it to be her breakthrough role, the one that proved that she could act. It was also her first

Marilyn Monroe listens intently to director John Huston on the set of Metro-Goldwyn-Mayer's *The Asphalt Jungle*. The film, which was released in 1950, was her first experience with a reputable cast and a well-known director. She remembered it fondly for the rest of her career.

role in an A-grade dramatic picture with a reputable director, John Huston, and cast, which included Louis Calhern, Sterling Hayden, and Sam Jaffe. *The Asphalt Jungle* was produced at MGM, and her friend and supporter Ryman, who worked in the talent department at the studio, as well as her agent, Hyde, believed she would be perfect for a minor role in the movie. Monroe worked fastidiously with her teacher Natasha Lytess in preparation for her audition for the role of Angela Phinlay, a young woman involved with a mob lawyer.

The film is a stark urban drama about an attempted jewelry robbery and reveals the hypocrisy of an underworld where criminals, police, and lawyers conspire together. Angela is the mistress of a married lawyer who organizes the robbery, though she is called his niece in the film, because the censorship code prohibited any reference to adulterous relationships. In her three scenes, Monroe reveals the delicate balance of youthful naïveté, sexual sophistication, and material greed in her character. She is sweet, charming, and as skittery as a scared rabbit when the police come to question her. Called "the crime picture of this decade" by the *New York Post, The Asphalt Jungle,* released in 1950, was the movie that made people notice Monroe. As *Photoplay* magazine put it: "There's a beautiful blonde, too, name of Marilyn Monroe, who plays Calhern's girlfriend, and makes the most of her footage."

Monroe herself would always consider this role as one of her best and most notable performances, and was grateful for the opportunity to work on a quality film with a reputable director. She said later, "Even though my part was a minor one, I felt as if I were the most important performer in the picture—when I was before the camera. This was because everything I did was important to the director, just as important as everything the stars of the picture did."

After *The Asphalt Jungle,* Monroe got small roles in three forgettable films: *The Fireball,* a Twentieth Century–Fox comedy starring Mickey Rooney; and *Right Cross* and *Home Town Story,* two MGM dramas. But then came another watershed role in a movie that went on to win six Academy Awards, including the Oscar for Best Picture. *All About Eve* was written and directed by Joseph L. Mankiewicz and featured an all-star cast in a biting script about Eve, a conniving young actress making her way to the top of the theater world. Anne Baxter played the title role in the film, which starred Bette Davis, Celeste Holm, George Sanders, Gary Merrill, and Thelma Ritter. Once again, Monroe's role was small but significant. She played Miss Caswell, graduate of the Copacabana School of Dramatic Art, who befriends a powerful critic (played by Sanders) in the hope of furthering her career. The character of Miss Caswell works as a dramatic foil to the Eve character, as Miss Caswell openly displays her ambitions and talents, which lie more in her looks than in her acting abilities. The film's critical and popular success meant visibility for Monroe, even though her role was small and one-dimensional. By the end of 1950—still without a studio contract—Monroe had a growing reputation as a starlet with potential.

5 The Making of an Icon

BY 1951, MARILYN MONROE had become a noticeable presence in Hollywood and was attracting considerable publicity. She appeared not only in the popular films *The Asphalt Jungle* and *All About Eve,* but also in widely read magazines such as *Life* and *Look,* where her photographs generated immense interest. Her agent and friend Johnny Hyde, who died in December 1950, had helped increase Monroe's visibility, and Twentieth Century–Fox soon recognized her new popularity by offering Monroe a long-term contract. Effective May 11, 1951, it was a standard seven-year contract, paying $500 a week for the first year, with yearly incremental raises should the studio opt to renew it at the end of the year. The one unique clause in the contract stated that Fox would pay for the services of Natasha Lytess as Monroe's drama coach.

Monroe's contract with Fox signified the end of her days as a starlet, when she hoped to be noticed and cast in movies, and it marked the beginning of her rise to full-fledged star, with a plethora of publicity and movie roles. It is no coincidence that Monroe's rise to stardom came in the 1950s, a decade

---

The 1954 wedding of Hollywood's favorite star Marilyn Monroe and former New York Yankees outfielder "Joltin'" Joe DiMaggio created headlines all over the world. The couple's marriage, which was tumultuous, lasted only nine months, partly because of Monroe's commitment to her career.

characterized by abundance and prosperity. Not everyone in postwar America prospered: economic distress affected significant portions of the population, and racism, which prevented African Americans from voting in many states, was rampant. But in the first postwar decade, the white middle class was growing and moving to the suburbs, and those who could afford to ignore the country's problems did. The war and postwar years were the first since the 1920s in which jobs and wages were on the increase, though these raises did not evenly affect every segment of the population. The economic conditions meant a rise in consumerism, helped along by the invention of the television (which brought commercials into the home) and the manufacturing of a host of new appliances. Though life was not as rosy as it was portrayed on television programs such as "Father Knows Best" and "Leave It to Beaver," this decade has become linked with symbols of fun, lightness, and prosperity. Monroe, whose public image was a unique combination of innocence, daring, and glamour, became another "feel-good" symbol of the times, as appealing as the new cars, jukeboxes, bobby-soxers, drive-ins, and rock-and-roll music.

In contrast to her first signing with Twentieth Century–Fox in 1946, this time Monroe did not have to wait long between assignments. In *As Young as You Feel,* (which was actually made before her seven-year deal) she played a secretary in a light comedy-drama about a forced retirement at a printing company. In *Love Nest,* another comedy, she played a former Wac (member of the Women's Army Corps) who stirs up jealous feelings when she moves into an apartment building owned by a young married couple. And in *Let's Make It Legal,* yet another forgettable comedy, she played a woman looking for a rich man to marry. In these roles, which were small and relied heavily on Monroe's looks, she played one of two types: either the dumb blonde or the conniving blonde.

For her next film project, her fourth of 1951, Fox loaned Monroe out to another studio, RKO. This practice of borrowing and loaning contract actors was common under the studio system, though a more accurate term would be "renting," because the home studio charged the borrowing one for the use of the actor (without, of course, passing the profit on to the actor). The RKO motion picture *Clash by Night* was a first-class project based on a drama by American playwright Clifford Odets, directed by the renowned Austrian-born director Fritz Lang (who had risen to fame for his films *M* and *Metropolis* in pre–World War II Germany), and starring popular actress Barbara Stanwyck. The role of Peggy, a fish cannery worker, was a departure from the spate of stereotypical blondes that Monroe had been playing. Peggy is down-to-earth, energetic, and not afraid to stand up to her fiancé. Though the role was small, she was noticed and praised in the reviews. "Before going any further with a report on *Clash by Night*," said the *New York World Telegram and Sun*, "perhaps we should mention the first full-length glimpse the picture gives us of Marilyn Monroe as an actress. . . . She has definitely stamped herself as a gifted new star, worthy of all that fantastic press agentry. Her role here is not very big but she makes it dominant." James Monaco, in his 1992 book *The Movie Guide*, said this about Monroe's performance: "This is the lovely Monroe without the candy floss accoutrements: one watches *Clash* sensing her career might have gone in a totally different direction had Fox marketed her in an adult manner."

However, those who worked with Monroe on *Clash by Night* offer a glimpse of the actress that did not show on the screen. According to director Lang, she was "scared as hell to come to the studio, always late, couldn't remember her lines and was certainly responsible for slowing down the work." Stanwyck noted that "She was awkward. She couldn't get out of her own way. She wasn't disciplined . . . and she drove Bob Ryan, Paul Douglas and myself out of our minds . . . but she didn't do it viciously, and there was a sort of magic about her which we all recognized at once."

Monroe, who had begun to develop a reputation for lateness back in her days on *All About Eve*, was often overcome with nervousness, stemming from her acute perfectionism. Marjorie Plecher, who worked in the studio's wardrobe department, offered this insight: "She never felt secure in front of the cameras. She was so scared about looking right, acting right, that she was physically unable to leave the trailer. It was the ultimate stage fright. She had a great talent, but she never felt sure of herself, never could believe in herself." Her nervousness and lateness often held up bigger stars and directors, who were not always so understanding or tolerant.

Along with her lateness, another of Monroe's working habits that became part of her reputation was her dependency on her drama coach. As far back as *The Asphalt Jungle,* Monroe had arranged for Lytess to work with her on the set during filming. Needless to say, the presence of an acting coach, especially for an actor in a minor role, often irritated the director. Fritz Lang minced no words in describing his views: "I do not want anyone directing behind my back. I want this Lytess woman kept off my set." He was not the first director who had a problem with Monroe's coach, and he would not be the last. But Monroe would not work without her coach. Though Lytess may or may not have been essential to Monroe's successful performances, for many years Monroe certainly believed that Lytess was indispensable. As the actress Shelley Winters, a friend of Monroe's, explained, "Marilyn had very little self worth. She didn't trust that she could do something by herself. And so very early in her career she began to get coaches."

60

In any case, Monroe completed a noteworthy performance in *Clash by Night,* and even before its release the positive reviews were circulating around her home studio. So, for the first time since the B-grade musical *Ladies of the Chorus,* Twentieth Century–Fox cast Monroe in a starring role. In *Don't Bother To Knock,* a low-budget melodrama with Richard Widmark and Anne Bancroft, Monroe played Nell, a mentally unstable hotel baby-sitter. Nell, who convinces herself that one of the hotel guests is actually her fiancé who died in the war, was another divergence from the shallow sexy characters Monroe generally played. Her portrayal takes Nell from being a competent and shy baby-sitter to being increasingly needy, unstable, cruel, and finally, frightening. The reviews were mixed, both of the film and of Monroe's performance, but the role was an important stepping-stone in her career, because it showed she could carry a film well enough to attract an audience. Furthermore, near the time of its release in July 1952, Monroe was the subject of an intense media campaign, and her name and picture had appeared all over the place. At this point, any film she acted in would have attracted attention.

Publicity has been an integral part of the movies since their invention. In the early 1900s, when the novelty of moving pictures was its biggest attraction, the names of actors did not appear in the movies or in any advertisements for them. But by the 1920s, movie producers had realized that the public paid attention to particular actors, and by revealing those actors' names and announcing them in advertisements, the producers could generate interest in a movie. This technique was the beginning of the star system, which acknowledged the ability of a recognizable name to draw audiences to the movie theater and thus make money. A star was an actor whose name was well known enough to appear before the title of the film. The star system also cemented the relationship between the press and the movies, which have been symbiotically supporting and depending on each other ever since. One of the first discoveries made by the press and the film companies was that the public liked knowing about the personal lives of the screen stars. Soon the film companies established entire departments whose sole purpose was to generate publicity, invent offscreen lives for its stars, and feed this information to newspapers and magazines.

By the time that Marilyn Monroe was rising to success in the 1950s, the power of the press had become enormous, with movie columnists like Hedda Hopper, Louella Parsons, and Sidney Skolsky as feared and revered as anyone in Hollywood. Monroe, who had been involved in studio publicity maneuvers since her early days as a contract player, understood the role of good publicity in her quest for stardom. Through either good fortune or a cunning pragmatism, she befriended these columnists and secured their help in promoting her. One of the myths about Monroe concerns her relationship with the press. Views differ on whether she was a victim or master of the press: a clever manipulator who used the press to further her career, or the innocent prey of the publicity machinery. But no one denies that Monroe and the media are inextricably linked and that the story of Marilyn Monroe the movie star is in many ways the story of Marilyn Monroe the media star. At this point in her career, when she was trying to establish herself, she welcomed the chance to be interviewed or photographed for newspapers and magazines, in part because the visibility increased her chances of getting bigger and better movie roles. "I think cheesecake helps call attention to you," she said in 1951. "Then you can follow through and prove yourself."

An integral part of the publicity machinery was the studio's own publicity departments, which created names, ages, and personal histories for its contracted actors. These studio biographies often exaggerated or even invented events in order to make an interesting story. "From lonely orphan to sought after motion picture star is the true life Cinderella story of Marilyn Monroe," is how one studio-issued biography of Monroe reads. It goes on to claim that she never knew either of her parents and once lived in a home where her only friends were a collection of exotic birds! This rags-to-riches story of Monroe's life, part truth and part fiction, would follow her around for the rest of her life. Another biography, issued a few years later, also capitalized on the fairy-tale elements of her story: "Roll all the Cinderella stories into one. Summon up the copy writer's extravagant superlatives. Take the drama and pathos from the greatest novels. Stand her beside the loveliest beauties of all time. Do all these things and they won't compare with the Hollywood phenomenon, Marilyn Monroe, whose sudden fame and frenetic following have never been equalled in or out of motion pictures." Such press releases, as well as her movie roles, created a public image of Monroe as a helplessly sexy, hopelessly innocent waif, who loved the adoration but did not quite know what all the fuss was about.

In 1952, the press made two discoveries that threatened to undermine this image of Monroe. In each case she was able to maneuver them from being potential scandals to becoming positive publicity, coups that have added to the myth of Monroe's handling of the press. Back in May 1949, after Monroe had been dropped from both Twentieth Century–Fox and Columbia Pictures, she posed nude for photographs that were then used on two calendars, entitled "Golden Dreams" and "A New Wrinkle." As Monroe was becoming famous a few years later, when *Don't Bother To Knock* was opening in theaters, the press found out about the calendars. Though sex was a big part of Monroe's movie roles and her image in the press, full nudity was considered too extreme. Studio executives, who feared that the news about the nude calendar would harm the image of their promising new star, urged Monroe to deny that it was she in the picture. Instead, Monroe went directly to reporter Aline Mosby, who had uncovered the story, and explained why she had posed nude. In a move that is often cited as evidence of Monroe's knack for dealing with the press, Monroe impressed Mosby with her honesty and directness.

"A photograph of a beautiful nude blonde on a 1952 calendar is hanging in garages and barbershops all over the nation today," Mosby's story read. "Marilyn Monroe admitted today that the beauty is she." The article quotes Monroe as saying, "Why deny it? I've done nothing wrong. . . . I was a week behind on my rent. I had to have the money." By reinforcing the image of Monroe as "another scared young blonde, struggling to find fame in the magic city, and all alone," the article encouraged the public's sympathy. When the article appeared in papers around the country, it increased, rather than diminished, Monroe's popularity.

Not three months later, another potential scandal broke, this one concerning Monroe's status as an orphan. Once again Monroe was able to deflect the controversy. As reported by Erskine Johnson in May 1952, "Hollywood's confessin' glamour doll who made recent headlines with the admission that she was a nude calendar cutie confessed again today." Upon discovering that Monroe's mother was alive and living in an institution, Johnson and others confronted Monroe with her claim that she was an orphan. Monroe responded by telling of her mother's hospitalization and stating that "I haven't known my mother intimately but since I have become grown and able to help her, I have contacted her." Indeed, though she had no personal contact with her mother for some five years, she had, since her income had increased, been contributing to her mother's care. At first the news threatened to undermine the Cinderella image of Monroe that the studio and press had been building up for years. But again, her directness and compassion swayed public sympathy her way.

The result of all this publicity was to make Monroe more in demand at the studio. She appeared in five pictures released in 1952 and was now routinely working with established stars. Monroe, however, rarely got the chance to stretch beyond the role of a dumb blonde. As Kate Cameron wrote in a *New York Daily News* review, Monroe "can look and act dumber than any of the screen's current blondes." In the comedy *We're Not Married,* with Ginger Rogers, Eve Arden, and Zsa Zsa Gabor, she played a beauty contestant. In another comedy, *Monkey Business,* with Cary Grant, Ginger Rogers, and a chimpanzee, she played a secretary. And in O. Henry's *Full House,* which was based on five stories by him, Monroe has a small scene as a streetwalker with veteran actor Charles Laughton. Though Monroe appeared for approximately one minute in the film, she received star billing when it was released. The studio executives had obviously learned that Marilyn Monroe was a name that could draw audiences to the box office.

Following this reasoning, they finally put her in a starring role in a high-visibility drama. *Niagara,* released in January 1953, was a breakthrough role for Monroe. A sultry thriller set in New York State's Niagara Falls, the film was directed by the eminent Henry Hathaway and featured Monroe as Rose Loomis, an adulterous wife who plots to have her husband (played by Joseph Cotten) killed. As critic Otis L. Guernsey, Jr., wrote in the *New York Herald Tribune,* "Miss Monroe plays the kind of wife whose dress, in the words of the script, 'is cut so low you can see her knees.' The dress is red; the actress has

Marilyn Monroe and Jane Russell, costars in *Gentlemen Prefer Blondes*, place their handprints in the wet cement in front of Hollywood's Grauman's Chinese Theater on June 26, 1953. Monroe's fame had reached the point where the press covered everything she did.

very nice knees, and under Hathaway's direction she gives the kind of serpentine performance that makes the audience hate her while admiring her, which is proper for the story."

One of the most famous scenes in *Niagara* features a long shot of Monroe, as Loomis, walking on the grounds of the Niagara Falls motel where she is staying with her husband. Though her walk had been featured in *Love Happy*, it was in this shot that it became famous. And like many other facets of Monroe's mystique, her sexy stride became a subject of controversy and debate. For years people have put forth theories on how she walked and why she walked that way. Some claim that she was double-jointed and had locked knees, or that a swimming accident or a childhood fall had left her with a weak ankle. Others accused her of contriving her sexy walk, along with everything else in her career, to add to her popularity. Some even claim that she engineered it by cutting off a quarter inch from one shoe heel to make her lopsided. And then there are those that said it came from the simple combination of her high heels and the uneven cobblestone pavement. Monroe always claimed it was her natural walk. "People say I walk all wiggly and wobbly, but I don't know what they mean," she said later. "I've never wiggled deliberately in my life, but all my life I've had trouble with people who say I do. . . . I learned to walk when I was ten months old and I've been walking this way ever since."

Though *Niagara* generated more publicity for Monroe, it was her next film, *Gentlemen Prefer Blondes,* released later that year, that firmly established her as a star. Based on the book and Broadway musical by Anita Loos, *Gentlemen Prefer Blondes* starred Jane Russell as Dorothy and Monroe as Lorelei Lee, two glamorous entertainers in search of husbands. Monroe hoped the movie, directed by Howard Hawks, would secure her place as a star and prepared diligently for her performance. She worked with her coach Natasha Lytess on the dramatic scenes, and with choreographer Jack Cole and the studio musicians on the song and dance numbers. She had several musical numbers, including "Two Little Girls from Little Rock," with Russell, and "Diamonds Are a Girl's Best Friend," which became her signature song. In this routine, which is one of Monroe's most famous, she wears a red strapless gown and, of course, diamonds. Surrounded by a swarm of men in tuxedos, she oozes sex and pragmatism and sings about the importance of getting material goods in a love affair.

Monroe's performance in *Gentlemen Prefer Blondes,*
which helped make the movie a hit at the box office,
showcased her talents for comedy and singing. Her portrayal of Lorelei was an endearing and comical caricature
of unabashed materialism. Monroe used seductiveness,
sultry singing, and her ability to poke fun at the character
she was playing to create her most popular role to date.
To capitalize on this popularity, the studio assigned
Monroe to a similar role in *How To Marry a Millionaire,*
with Lauren Bacall and Betty Grable. With a plot line
reminiscent of *Blondes,* the film concerns three glamorous
models and their search for suitable (that is, rich) husbands. Monroe, as the nearsighted Pola, once again showcased her talent for comedy. The *New York Post's* review
stated that "Miss Monroe has developed more than a
small amount of comedy polish of the foot-in-mouth
type" and commended her performance as "a compara-
tive innocent who smiles at anything in the hopes it might
be masculine. Since she doesn't want to be seen wearing
glasses, she can never be sure."

In 1953, Monroe, along with costar Jane Russell,
added her handprints to the sidewalk of Grauman's Chinese Theater in Hollywood, making her stardom official.
By now, her fame had reached the point where everything
she did was a media event. She attended premieres,
parties, and award ceremonies, often in risqué dresses that
garnered her even more publicity. Her picture appeared
on the cover of dozens of magazines, including *Collier's,
Life, Laff, Peek, Photoplay,* and *Quick.* She appeared on
"The Jack Benny Show" on television and was featured
in magazine advertisements. She was named Miss
Cheesecake of 1951 by the U.S. Army magazine *Stars and
Stripes*; Fastest Rising Star of 1952 by *Photoplay* magazine; and Best Young Box Office Personality by *Redbook*
magazine in 1953; and served as the grand marshal of the
Miss America Parade in 1952. Though not her most

prestigious honor, one of her most telling was being named Most Advertised Girl in the World by the Advertising Association of the West in 1953.

For Monroe, this success was a reward for her years of diligence and patience: her lessons in singing, dancing, and acting; her work with her drama coach, Natasha Lytess; and her lessons with other instructors, such as mime Lotte Goslar and actor Michael Chekhov, who was trained by the great Russian actor-director, Konstantin Stanislavsky. Monroe, who never felt supported by Darryl F. Zanuck or the other executives at Twentieth Century–Fox, always gave the credit for her stardom to the public. "If I am a star, the people made me a star," she said. "There was no studio and no person. The people made me a star." Actress Shelley Winters, who used to "sit in Schwab's Drugstore and fantasize about the future" with Monroe, remembered the coming of her success as "the most glorious and wonderful thing."

But at the same time that Monroe was enjoying the pleasures of fame, she was beginning to experience the drawbacks, in both the personal and the professional aspects of her life. With almost everything she did or said reported in the news, Monroe had no privacy. "They're kind of grabbing pieces out of you," she said once about reporters. "And gee, you do want to stay intact."

Just as frustrating was that all the publicity—the articles and photographs, as well as her film roles—projected a one-sided view of her as a brainless sex goddess. To Monroe, the sex goddess was a role that she portrayed in films, in photographs, and at public appearances. As her friend actor Robert Mitchum explained, her attitude toward being a "sex goddess or glamour queen" was that "she would play it if that's what they wanted." Though her sexuality was certainly a part of her personality, it was only one part. Yet it seemed to be the only part that the studio or the press could see. As Winters said years later,

"You don't realize when you make these deals early in your life, and she certainly did, with publicity, that you have to live with them forever."

But the most frustrating result of her public image was that it limited her choice of film roles. The catch-22 for Monroe was that her portrayal of characters like the shallow, sexy Lorelei Lee was so convincing that the studio executives, the press, and the public could not see her as anything else. It was standard during the studio era for production executives to develop stars as certain types, gearing publicity and casting toward reinforcing that image of the star. It was also common for the actors to be frustrated by this typecasting. Monroe, like many actors before and during her time, wanted a chance to develop her skills and range as an actress. She wanted to be taken seriously, and she wanted to be cast in roles outside of the dumb sex goddess type. The studio, however, was satisfied to keep her playing the same kind of character because it had proven successful at the box office.

Following this line of thinking, production executives next assigned her to the role of a saloon singer in a Western called *River of No Return*. Though the project involved a reputable director, Otto Preminger, and co-star, Robert Mitchum, Monroe was dissatisfied with the script. Shot mostly on location in the Canadian Rockies, the film became an exhausting disaster for Monroe, who did not get along well with Preminger. Upon its release, the film got mixed-to-poor reviews, which focused mainly on the scenery and the use of the new wide-screen filming process of CinemaScope. Monroe's frustration had come to a head. "Knowing what I know now," she said after the film was released. "I wouldn't accept *River of No Return*. I think I deserve a better deal than a 'Z' cowboy movie, in which the acting finishes third to the scenery and CinemaScope."

Apparently the studio still did not take Monroe's concerns seriously. Her next assignment was *The Girl in Pink Tights,* another light musical comedy that called for her to simply replicate the same type she had made famous in her other movies. This time, however, Monroe refused to do the movie. "I read the script and didn't like it," she said. "The part isn't good for me. It's as simple as that." The studio then suspended Monroe, as it had done over the years with other contract actors who did not report to their assigned project. But she was too popular to leave dangling for long, and soon Monroe and the studio negotiated a compromise, which included a salary adjustment to reflect her higher earning power as well as permission not to do the proposed movie. She also consented to a role in another musical, *There's No Business Like Show Business,* released in 1954, that was very much in line with her usual characters and included a scene in which, according to film scholar James Monaco, Monroe "[turned] up the temperature with her sexy rendition of 'Heat Wave.'" In exchange for playing this role, she received the starring role in a coveted script called *The Seven Year Itch,* which was being developed.

While Monroe spent most of her time in the early 1950s working on her career, she also had a personal life. Of course, when the fastest-rising movie star in the country marries one of the most famous American sports figures, it is hard to keep the relationship private. Early in 1952, "Joltin'" Joe DiMaggio, recently retired from the New York Yankees baseball team, asked a mutual friend to introduce him to Monroe. She reluctantly agreed to meet him and several friends for dinner. "I was surprised to be so crazy about Joe," she said later. "I expected a flashy New York sports type, and instead I met this reserved guy who didn't make a pass at me right away. I had dinner with him almost every night for two weeks. He treated me like something special. Joe is a very decent

While in Japan with DiMaggio, Monroe accepted an invitation to perform for the U.S. troops stationed in Korea. It was a rare live performance for Monroe, who later said, "It was the highlight of my life." Here Monroe talks to the soldiers as one gleefully touches her toe.

man, and he makes other people feel decent, too." Two years later, on January 14, 1954, in an act that fortified the fairy-tale aura of Monroe's life, she and DiMaggio were married. The public interest in the marriage was enormous, and reporters and photographers followed them avidly.

A few weeks later, while Monroe was on suspension from her studio, the newlyweds went to Japan with some friends of theirs. The primary purpose of the trip was for DiMaggio to attend a series of baseball exhibition games in Japan, where the sport was rapidly becoming popular. Crowds of people and hordes of reporters and photographers greeted the couple wherever they went in Japan. At a press conference staged primarily for Joe, many of the questions were directed at Monroe. Her responses demonstrated her unique wit and endearing style. When asked what kind of fur she was wearing, for example, she replied, "Fox—and not the Twentieth Century kind."

While in Japan, Monroe received an invitation to perform for the U.S. Army troops stationed in Korea. While DiMaggio stayed in Japan, she spent four days in Korea, on outdoor stages before thousands of soldiers, performing songs such as "Diamonds Are a Girl's Best Friend" and "Do It Again." She had rarely performed in front of a live audience, and she found the experience exhilarating. "The highlight of my life," she said later, "was singing for the soldiers there. I stood out on an open stage and it was cold, but I swear I didn't feel anything but good." After returning to Japan, she tried to express her excitement to her husband: "Joe," she asked him, "do you have any idea what that's like? To have ten thousand people stand up and applaud you?" DiMaggio, who had hit plenty of home runs in Yankee Stadium, is reported to have responded "Yes. Seventy-five thousand."

The marriage was difficult from the start. Monroe, who had once said, "A career is wonderful, but you can't curl up with it on a cold night," nonetheless was dedicated to her profession. DiMaggio, for his part, may have made unrealistic assumptions about what a marriage to the most popular sex symbol in the world actually entailed. "It's no fun being married to an electric light," he said later. There is some speculation that he disapproved of her work and expected her to quit once they got married. Of all the family, friends, and colleagues of

Monroe's, DiMaggio is the only person who has never spoken to the press about her. But according to Whitey Snyder, who was a friend to both of them, "They loved one another, but they couldn't be married to one another." Before the year was out, Monroe had filed for divorce. In her statement to the judge, she cited DiMaggio's "coldness and indifference" among the reasons for her divorce plea. The media coverage of the divorce was as extensive as it had been for the wedding. The two remained friends, however, and saw each other frequently.

Monroe closed out the first half of the decade with a film that became one of her most popular. *The Seven Year Itch,* directed by Billy Wilder and costarring Tom Ewell,

A tearful Monroe, clenching a handkerchief, stoically answers reporters' questions as she leaves her and DiMaggio's Beverly Hills home. Although they came from similar backgrounds (neither completed high school and both desired to rise above their humble beginnings), Monroe and DiMaggio were two very different people with separate goals; their marriage officially ended in October 1954.

Larger than life, a 52-foot Marilyn Monroe towers above New York City's Times Square, advertising the June 1955 release of *The Seven Year Itch*. The scene from the movie of Monroe standing over a subway grate with her skirt blowing up is one of her most famous.

started filming almost immediately after Monroe completed the work on *There's No Business Like Show Business*. The comedy features Monroe as a charming and naive upstairs neighbor to a shy man who has been married for seven years and whose family is on vacation for the summer. Though sex and naïveté were big parts of her role in *The Seven Year Itch,* this movie had more depth and sophistication than her earlier musicals and offered

Monroe another chance to demonstrate her talent for comedy. As The Girl, she plays off the jittery, neurotic neighbor, portrayed by Ewell, who constantly fantasizes about having an affair with her. She delivers her lines, which are filled with double entendres, with a deftness that makes the double meanings elude her character but reach the audience.

The most famous image from the movie, indeed one of the most famous of her career, is of Monroe standing on a subway grate on a New York City street. Wearing a white summer dress, Monroe steps onto the grate to catch the breeze of a subway passing below. "Isn't it delicious?" she coos, as the breeze blows at her dress, inadvertently revealing much of her legs. The filming was staged at 2:00 A.M. on the streets of Manhattan, where thousands of New Yorkers gathered to watch it. This staging was primarily for publicity, however, as the shot had to be refilmed in its entirety back at the studio in Hollywood. As a publicity stunt it was very successful, and the picture of Monroe with her dress fluttering up around her shoulders was enlarged and reproduced on billboards and in advertisements across the country. Upon its release in 1955, *The Seven Year Itch* became a box office smash, and today it is one of her most well-known movies.

6 ★ The New Marilyn

AFTER A STEADY RISE TO STARDOM in the early 1950s, Marilyn Monroe soon reached the peak of fame and popularity. She then surprised everyone by leaving Hollywood. To the press and the public, Monroe's move to New York City at the end of 1954 came as a shock. But a look at the many reasons behind her move makes neither the decision nor the timing surprising at all. Monroe's decision reflected her growing dissatisfaction with her public image and with the press and studio that perpetuated that image. It reflected her desire to develop her acting skills so that she could tackle dramatic film roles with confidence. She also simply needed a well-deserved break. For the past several years, she had maintained a hectic pace, often barely finishing a film before being whisked into the next one.

Many forces had contributed to Monroe's image of glamour and sexiness, including the studio, the press, the public, and Monroe herself. But by the mid-1950s, the image was stifling, as was the media attention that had propelled her to worldwide fame. The pressure of maintaining the image of the sex goddess was overwhelming. As actor Robert Wagner explained, "It

---

On June 29, 1956, in what newspapers dubbed the union of "the Egghead and the Hourglass," Marilyn Monroe married her third husband, Pulitzer Prize–winning playwright Arthur Miller.

just didn't happen real easy. She just didn't walk on a set and they said 'Roll 'em' and she did it. It took a lot of time, a lot of rehearsing, to create that whole image." And at this point in her career, Monroe was tired of working so hard for an image that represented only one side of her. As playwright Arthur Miller, a friend of Monroe's in New York (and later her husband), explained, "She could hardly find a sentence in any [news article] about her, even those written in praise, that was not condescending at best, and the majority seemed to have been written by slavering imbeciles who liked to pretend that her witty sexuality marked her as little better than a whore, and a dumb one at that." Monroe was disappointed with the press and told her personal publicist at the time, "I'm so sick of being treated like a thing."

But Monroe's biggest complaints were with her studio, Twentieth Century–Fox, which continued to cast her in roles that perpetuated the very image she was trying to alter. After a string of successful films, she felt she deserved more complex and less stereotyped roles. In this light, the timing of Monroe's hiatus from Hollywood is understandable, especially after the release of *The Seven Year Itch,* when she had reached a pinnacle of popularity. That popularity, which translated into earning power at the box office, put her in a strong position to negotiate with the studio. As a starlet, she had been grateful for any role offered her, but now, as a full-fledged star, she wanted some say in her roles. And the studio executives now had to listen. Four years into the long-term contract she had signed with the studio in 1951, Monroe's quick rise to success had made the contract out of date, in terms of both her salary and her decision-making power.

Monroe's contract renegotiations actually started before she left for New York. In 1954, she and her friend Milton Greene, a photographer, began the legal process to start a company called Marilyn Monroe Productions.

With Monroe as president and Greene as vice-president, the two established the company to give Monroe more autonomy in her career. Marilyn Monroe Productions was to work in conjunction with Twentieth Century–Fox to develop film projects for Monroe. It would give her a vehicle to take part in the production of her movies by giving her a voice in the selection of scripts, actors, and directors. On January 7, 1955, at a New York City press conference, Monroe and Greene announced the formation of their new company. Monroe, who refused to make another film until the negotiations with the studio were settled, was effectively on strike. As she later explained, "My fight with the studio is not about money. It is about human rights. I am tired of being known as the girl with the shape. I am going to show that I am capable of deeper acting." Later, in an appearance on the television program "Person to Person," broadcaster Edward R. Murrow interviewed Monroe, Greene, and Greene's wife, Amy, at the Greene home in Connecticut, where Monroe was a house guest. "Would it be fair to say you got rather tired of playing the same roles all the time and would like to try something different?" Murrow asked her. "It's not that I object to doing musicals or comedies," she responded. "In fact I rather enjoy it. But I would like to do also dramatic parts."

For much of 1955, lawyers representing Monroe and her company negotiated with the lawyers from the studio for a contract that would satisfy both sides. When the negotiations were complete, after about a year, Monroe signed with Twentieth Century–Fox under much better terms. Among them was an increase in salary that brought her closer to what other stars of her stature were making and a bonus of $100,000 that Fox had promised her for her work on *The Seven Year Itch*. In addition, she would be able to work at a more reasonable pace because she would be committed to only four films over the next seven years. Most important to Monroe, she won a voice in choosing scripts, directors, and cinematographers: from this point on Monroe would be able to approve all three before she started a film.

Monroe was not the first movie star to fight with her studio, but as Hollywood's studio era was coming to an end in the 1950s, her strong stance and eventual victory signified and added to the changes in the system and the growing power of the actor. Although she was very much a product of the studio and star systems, she arrived at the tail end of their reign in Hollywood, and the changes in her career reflect the transitions taking place. By the time she started her production company and began negotiations with her studio, she was one of many actors who had become fed up with studio executives typecasting them and telling them how to act, both on-screen and offscreen.

The authority of the studio system had been weakening for a decade, and Monroe's "strike" came when it was at the point of disintegration. One factor contributing to this crumbling of the system was economic. The power of the studios had always come from their strength at the box office. Going to the movies was a very popular form of entertainment, even in hard times. Indeed, the movie industry was one of the few to do well during the Great Depression. But by the mid-1950s, film industry profits dropped dramatically: from 1950 to 1956 they fell by $200 million. Changing economic times, as well as the advent of television, and to a lesser extent radio, meant fewer people were going to the movies. During World War II, movie theaters had thriving audiences, but in the 1950s theaters had to resort to gimmicks, such as bingo games and dish giveaways, to attract customers.

Meanwhile, a series of court cases had declared the very structure of the studio system to be illegal. In 1949, in *The United States vs. Paramount, Inc.,* the U.S. Supreme

Court decided that antimonopoly laws prohibited a corporation from owning both the means of production and the means of exhibition. All of the movie theaters in the country were either owned by one of the Big Five film companies or dependent on them for obtaining movies. The Big Five thus had enough money and power to keep most competitors out of both ends of the movie business. With hardly any other companies making and distributing films, they could tell theaters what movies to show and how long to show them, regardless of how popular the movies were. But the Supreme Court ruling curtailed the power of the Big Five by breaking up their monopolies and opening up the film industry to competitors. By 1954, the studios had divested themselves of their theater holdings and had lost a great deal of their earning power as a result.

The shrinking audiences, the decreasing profits, and the breakup of the monopolies were all factors in the dissolution of the studio system of movie production. During the 1950s and 1960s, the film corporations underwent major restructuring as mergers, divestments, and takeovers took place. The movie moguls who had once been feared and revered lost their power to new executives. By this time the studios could no longer afford to keep a whole staff of stars and technicians under long-term contract. Actors, directors, and producers began to form their own production companies, which worked in conjunction with the studios to produce movies on a per-picture basis. In these deals, the production companies supplied the talent, whereas the studio provided just the equipment and financing, followed by the distribution. Nowadays, when a major studio puts its name on a movie, it usually means that the studio has given money and some production guidance to a project developed by an independent company. Marilyn Monroe Productions was one of several companies formed during this transitional period in the American movie industry. And although Monroe's career was styled by the studio era, she was actually one of the last of its stars, because her career outlasted the system itself.

But challenging her public image, renegotiating with her studio, and starting her production company were not the only changes Monroe instigated in 1955. Her move to New York was also intended as a way to concentrate on the art and craft of acting. She immersed herself in theater, watching Broadway and off-Broadway productions, and enrolled in classes at the Actors Studio, which was founded by the actor-directors Cheryl Crawford, Robert Lewis, and Elia Kazan. By this time, the Studio was run by actor-director Lee Strasberg, who had been influenced by the teachings of Konstantin Stanislavsky. The Actors Studio was a major forum for serious actors in the 1950s— Paul Newman, Marlon Brando, and James Dean all came out of the Studio, as did, in later years, Robert de Niro, Jane Fonda, and Sally Field. Following Stanislavsky's emphasis on understanding character through motivation, Strasberg had developed an approach called the Method, in which actors use emotional recall to find the psychological motivations of

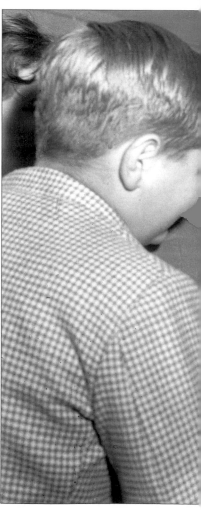

their characters. It relies heavily on improvisation in the rehearsal process and encourages the actor to undergo psychological analysis with a psychiatrist. "The idea is you learn to use everything that happened in your life in creating the character you're working on," explained Marlon Brando. "You learn to dig into your unconscious and make use of every experience you ever had."

But the Actors Studio and its Method were not without controversy. Many actors, from George C. Scott to

In 1956, Monroe signs autographs for young fans at New York's Idlewild Airport (later renamed John F. Kennedy International Airport). Monroe adored children and wanted one of her own, but she miscarried each time she tried.

Sir Laurence Olivier, criticized its emphasis on motivation and psychology and made fun of the typical dark, moody Method actor. And many were skeptical of Lee Strasberg, who was revered by the members of the Actors Studio and at times seemed to overstep his bounds as a teacher and mentor. His interest in psychology caused him to delve into intimate, and possibly inappropriate, levels with the Studio members. Elia Kazan, who knew both Strasberg and Monroe, said that the members of the Studio "enshrined" Strasberg. "The more naive and self-doubting the actors, the more total was Lee's power over them. The more famous and the more successful these actors, the headier the taste of power for Lee. He found his perfect victim-devotee in Marilyn Monroe."

The relationship between Monroe and Strasberg was to become as involved and intense as any of her relationships, and certainly as controversial. For Strasberg it was a coup to have a star of Monroe's stature come to him for help. First he gave her private lessons at his family's apartment, because he did not feel she was ready for the rigorous group work at the Studio. When she did go to the Studio, she went alone, with no fanfare. Feminist Gloria Steinem, who also attended these classes, remembers being "shocked at how different she was from the movie star image. She didn't seem to have any makeup on, she looked kind of luminous, but just enormously shy . . . sitting way at the back of the room just observing other actors do an exercise." Monroe quickly became devoted to the principles of the Method, and Strasberg became intertwined with her personal and professional life. It was on his advice that she began analysis with a psychiatrist.

As Monroe developed her acting skills, she and her partner, Milton Greene, were also developing film projects for their new company. Their first movie would be *Bus Stop,* which was based on a successful stage play. In the spring of 1956 Monroe returned to Hollywood to start work on the film. Her return was a media event, and the press clamored to get a glimpse of "The New Marilyn." At one news conference, a reporter asked Monroe about her changes. "When you left here last year you were dressed differently, Marilyn. Now you have a black dress and a high-necked blouse: is this the new Marilyn?" Monroe, getting a laugh, responded, "No, I'm the same person—it's just a new dress." Some in Hollywood ridiculed Monroe's acting aspirations. "Marilyn's whole success is she can't act," said Billy Wilder, who had directed her in *The Seven Year Itch*. Many critics rushed into print with articles and books that shared this attitude; one minor book, called *Will Acting Spoil Marilyn Monroe?* summed up the skepticism.

Surrounded by such skeptics, Monroe was under immense pressure to prove herself as an actress in *Bus Stop*. The film, which is about a small-town saloon singer named Cherie who meets a country rancher named Bo, was significant for many reasons. It was Monroe's first movie since leaving Hollywood, her first under the auspices of Marilyn Monroe Productions, and the first to involve her in producing aspects, including decisions about the script, the director, and the cast. The role of Cherie, a downtrodden but dignified chanteuse, was a departure from the glamour of Monroe's previous characters. She worked well with director Joshua Logan, who later called her "the most talented picture actress alive in her day." He was impressed by her preparations for the role, which included designing less-than-flattering costumes and makeup to make the character authentic and believable. According to Logan, Monroe accomplished a difficult feat for an actor by "playing Cherie in a tender area that lies between comedy and tragedy." Shot partly on location in Phoenix, Arizona, the filming was strenuous, especially for Monroe, who was involved in

Marilyn Monroe jokes around with her fiancé Arthur Miller and his dog, Hugo, in 1956, four days before their wedding. Many believed that it was Monroe's relationship with Miller that helped him weather the storm of controversy surrounding his appearance before the House Un-American Activities Committee (HUAC).

many aspects of the production in addition to her own performance.

When the movie was released in the summer of 1956, all of her hard work seemed worthwhile, as positive reviews proved Monroe's skeptics wrong. "Hold onto your chairs, everybody, and get set for a rattling surprise," said the *New York Times*. "Marilyn Monroe has finally proved herself an actress in *Bus Stop*. She and the picture are swell." The *Saturday Review* commended the film, which "effectively dispels once and for all the notion that she is merely a glamour personality, a shapely body with

tremulous lips and come-hither blue eyes," and applauded Monroe's midcareer changes. "Miss Monroe has accomplished what is unquestionably the most difficult feat for any film personality," wrote reviewer Arthur Knight. "She has submerged herself so completely in the role that one searches in vain for glimpses of the former calendar girl."

Bus Stop was also significant for being the first film since her early days that Monroe had made without her drama coach Natasha Lytess. Once she started working with Lee Strasberg and the Actors Studio, Monroe broke off her professional ties, as well as her personal relationship, with Lytess. The dismissal of Lytess, which was done in writing through one of Monroe's staff, was an abrupt ending to a complex relationship. She did not give up the habit of using a coach, however; Strasberg's wife, Paula, served as Lee's representative on set. Like her habit of being late, Monroe's use of acting coaches has long been the subject of controversy. Though many directors found it irritating to have the coaches on set, some have expressed gratitude at their calming effect on Monroe. Others felt that Monroe had consistently involved herself with domineering coaches and other advisers and mentors who took advantage of her. She answered these critics with the following explanation:

> Johnny Hyde was wonderful, but he was not my Svengali [an evil manipulator]. Natasha Lytess was not my Svengali. Milton Greene was not my Svengali. I'm nobody's slave and never have been. Nobody hypnotizes me to do this or that. Now they write that Lee Strasberg is my Svengali. . . . I believe in learning and developing myself. Why shouldn't I have a coach? I never had any acting experience before I went into the movies . . . [and] I never had the privilege of okaying any takes they do on me, contrary to what they may have told you. The directors have that power, not me. When you're in the hands of a good director, it's good. But I not only didn't have acting

experience, I worked in some pictures where I was directed by men who never directed before or didn't know a thing about character or motivation or how to speak lines. Do you ever see on the screen "This picture was directed by an ignorant director with no taste"? No, the public always blames the star. *Me.* I had directors so stupid all they can do is repeat the lines of the script like they're reading a timetable. So I didn't get help from them. I had to find it elsewhere.

Moving to New York, starting her own company, and returning to Hollywood as "The New Marilyn" were not the only changes Monroe made in her life at this time: she also got married again. In 1956, she married Arthur Miller, playwright and author of the Pulitzer Prize–winning *Death of a Salesman*. She and Miller had met a few years earlier and spent much of the last year together in New York. Miller, who was married with two children when he first met Monroe, moved briefly to Reno, Nevada, to obtain a divorce. The press took the marriage announcement as another opportunity to ridicule Monroe. Calling them "the Beauty and the Brain," "the Egghead and the Hourglass," and "America's foremost representatives of the body and the mind," the press deemed "the marriage of the pin-up girl of the age and the nation's foremost intellectual playwright" to be "preposterous."

The marriage also thrust Monroe into a new arena: politics. In 1938, the U.S. Congress had established a special committee, the House Un-American Activities Committee (HUAC), to investigate alleged Communists whose activities were considered a threat to American democracy. HUAC was initially intended to put a stop to what it called Communist propaganda, but it actually focused its attention on various artists, intellectuals, labor leaders, and liberals who were considered at the time to have unorthodox views. The witch-hunt for Communist sympathizers had its greatest advocate in Senator Joseph McCarthy, who zealously investigated so-called subversives when he became chairman of the Senate Permanent Investigating Subcommittee of the Government Operations Committee in 1953. McCarthyism, as this political attitude toward alleged subversives became known, grew out of the hostility of the cold war between the United States and the Soviet Union and represented the hysteria of American paranoia during the 1950s. HUAC targeted the Hollywood movie industry as a center of anti-American activity and accused many screenwriters, directors, and actors of participation in illegal and insurgent political acts. The studio executives, who feared being tainted with political scandal, blacklisted many of these accused filmmakers, often ending their careers. In 1956, HUAC, under the chairmanship of Representative Harold R. Velde, summoned Arthur Miller to Washington, D.C., to answer questions about his Communist affiliations. For refusing to "name names" and identify suspected Communists, he was cited for contempt of Congress. His stance was considered noble by many others, however, as he put himself at personal risk in order to demonstrate his beliefs in the liberties guaranteed in the Constitution. Miller's association with Marilyn Monroe, whose image was as American as apple pie, helped temper the controversy. Monroe made public statements in support of her husband and, despite warnings from her studio bosses, did not appear to be worried that his activities might affect her own career.

Shortly after the wedding, Miller accompanied Monroe to England, where she was beginning the second project produced by Marilyn Monroe Productions. The movie, *The Prince and the Showgirl,* had actually been announced at a press conference before the filming of *Bus Stop*. It was a newsworthy announcement because the project teamed Monroe with Sir Laurence Olivier, the

In October 1956, Monroe and Susan Strasberg, daughter of Lee and Paula Strasberg, talk with actor Sir Laurence Olivier. Monroe and Olivier starred in *The Prince and the Showgirl*, an unlikely pairing that Monroe hoped would increase her respectability among critics as an actress.

premier English actor and director, who was to direct the movie as well as costar. The script, a comedy based on a stage play, followed the relationship between a straight-forward showgirl and a grand duke during the early 1900s. The pairing of Monroe and Olivier gave the press yet another opportunity to poke fun at Monroe's aspirations as a serious actress. At the press conference, a strap holding up Monroe's dress broke, causing a sensation among the 200 reporters and photographers. This inci-

dent added yet another story to the legend of Monroe and her relationship with the press. The rumors have long circulated that she broke the strap on purpose in order to generate publicity, and the episode is often cited as evidence of her savvy with the press.

While in England, Monroe lived with her husband in a stately countryside mansion, attended the London theater, and was invited to meet Queen Elizabeth II. But other aspects of her four-month stay were more arduous. A host of conflicts arose between people in the various factions of the production company. Very quickly the relationship between Monroe and Olivier soured. Olivier, who had no respect for Method acting, could not tolerate the presence of Monroe's coach, Paula Strasberg, and at one point arranged for her to be barred from the set. Monroe, in turn, could not tolerate Olivier's disrespect, condescension, and his habit of referring to her as "sweetie." Her tendency to arrive late increased, which only made Olivier think less of her.

Meanwhile Miller had disagreements with Milton Greene, Monroe's business partner, and with the Strasbergs, whom he felt were taking advantage of Monroe financially and emotionally. Greene had a similar view of the Strasbergs, whom he believed were charging the company too much money. Both Greene and Miller

93

tried to mediate the conflicts between Monroe and Olivier, but to no avail. Under the stress of these conflicts, Monroe's relationships with her new husband and with her business partner deteriorated. Both she and Greene were using medication, supplied by Greene's doctor, to help alleviate the emotional strain. The drugs, however, seemed to exacerbate Monroe's problems and to contribute to her lateness. At one point both Lee Strasberg and Marianne Kris, Monroe's psychiatrist, were flown to England from New York to try to solve some of these problems.

The difficulties on *The Prince and the Showgirl* proved to be too much for Marilyn Monroe Productions. Though the film was released to decent reviews, Monroe and Greene would never work together again, and the company soon dissolved. Back in New York, Monroe resumed her lessons with Strasberg and helped Miller deal with the last of his legal matters with HUAC. In the summer of 1957, while they were living in Amagansett, an oceanside town on New York's Long Island, Monroe became pregnant. In August, however, she collapsed in pain and was rushed to a hospital. There doctors determined that she had an ectopic pregnancy, in which the fetus forms in a fallopian tube rather than in the uterus. This type of pregnancy is fatal for the fetus and dangerous for the mother. After losing the baby, Monroe stayed 10 days in the hospital before returning home.

Back in Amagansett, she and Miller, who began to work on a screenplay for her to star in, lived a slow-paced, low-profile lifestyle. They took walks on the beach and started negotiations to purchase a country home in nearby Roxbury, Connecticut. Except for 1954, when Monroe went on "strike" from Twentieth Century–Fox, this was the longest hiatus she had taken from Hollywood. She was, however, in constant contact with the producers at the studio and with her agents, discussing

★ 7 ★ Something's Got To Give

IN 1958, ALMOST TWO YEARS after her last studio film, Monroe returned to Hollywood to star in the comedy *Some Like It Hot.* In many ways this film reinforced the image that Monroe had worked so hard to leave behind. Her character, Sugar Kane, describes herself as "just dumb" and is reminiscent of the sexy naïveté of Lorelei Lee from *Gentlemen Prefer Blondes,* The Girl from *The Seven Year Itch,* and other early Monroe roles. But the project was too attractive to pass up. Cowritten by Billy Wilder, the acclaimed director who had worked with Monroe on *The Seven Year Itch,* the script had a fast-paced, twisting plot and clever dialogue loaded with double entendres.

Set during the Roaring Twenties of the prohibition era, the film follows Joe and Jerry, two musicians played by Tony Curtis and Jack Lemmon, who masquerade as women in order to join an all-female band. Their first glimpse of Sugar Kane is on a train platform, where the band is boarding for an engagement in Florida. "Josephine" and "Daphne," the Curtis and Lemmon characters, are having trouble adjusting to wearing high heels and skirts. Sugar walks by and scurries out of the way as two blasts of steam from the train

---

Monroe is seen here playing the character Sugar Kane in the comedy *Some Like It Hot,* which was released in March 1959. The film, costarring Jack Lemmon and Tony Curtis, became one of Monroe's most successful films. She won a Golden Globe Award for Best Actress.

almost hit her (a gimmick that Monroe suggested). Josephine and Daphne are mesmerized. "Look how she moves," says Daphne. "That's just like jello on springs. They must have some kind of built-in motor. I tell you it's a whole different sex!"

The tremendous on-screen chemistry between Monroe and the two male leads created a series of hilarious scenes. Soon after meeting Josephine, Sugar admits she has "a thing about saxophone players, especially tenor sax." When Josephine (Joe) steps closer to tell her, "I play tenor sax," Sugar replies, "Yeah, but you're a girl, thank goodness." She has had enough of musicians who leave her with nothing but "a tube of toothpaste, all squeezed out" and wants to find a millionaire in Florida. The most comical and famous scene from the movie involves Sugar hopping into Daphne's sleeping berth on the train while Daphne, in a nightgown, struggles to keep his identity hidden. Soon the entire band joins them in Daphne's sleeping compartment for a drinking party.

The offscreen chemistry, however, was not so successful. Though Monroe and Wilder had worked well together before, they now had some difficulties. Wilder, who thought the world of Monroe's talents as a comedian, had been one of the many to doubt her abilities as a serious actress and to question her associations with the Strasbergs and the Actors Studio. Paula Strasberg, as Monroe's permanent acting coach, was on the set for the duration of the filming. There were also tensions between Monroe and her costars, Lemmon and Curtis, who were often held up because of her lateness or the numerous takes she demanded. In addition, several problems that had developed during her last project resurfaced while filming *Some Like It Hot*. The troubles in her marriage with Miller continued, and she was caught in conflicts between factions of her colleagues, staff, and friends. Monroe continued to use pills, prescribed by various

doctors, to alleviate stress and combat her chronic insomnia. These sedatives included barbiturates that often made her groggy in the morning and caused her to arrive late to work, which then contributed to the struggles she had with the director and cast.

Monroe's tardiness, which originally grew out of her perfectionism and fear of not performing well, had become legendary. She was notorious for arriving late to everything: interviews, photo sessions, business meetings, social engagements, and, of course, to work. In a light moment, Wilder once said, "Her idea of time is different, that's all. I think maybe there's a little watchmaker in Zurich, Switzerland, he makes a living produc-

Paula Strasberg (right) coaches Monroe on the set of *Some Like It Hot*. Throughout her career, Monroe demanded that her coaches be allowed on the sets of her movies. Monroe's acting coaches gave her the security she needed during production, but most directors disliked the intrusion.

ing special watches only for Marilyn Monroe." By this point in her career, however, the pressures in her life, and the medications she used to relieve them, increased her tendency to arrive late. Wilder, whose statements on Monroe ran the gamut from gushing to cutting, also said, "I would rather have Marilyn Monroe two hours late than another actress an hour early. . . . [But] the question then arises: How do I feel about Marilyn Monroe *six* hours late?"

During the filming of *Some Like It Hot,* Monroe, who was so physically drained that she was hospitalized for one weekend, discovered that she was pregnant again. Though Miller flew out to comfort her, he did not seem to alleviate the tension. Initially, she had admired Miller for his intellect and his sensitivity. But since their marriage, she had often been disappointed by the way he treated her. Her costar Jack Lemmon recognized later that she was "going through some kind of hell on earth—suffering and still producing that magic on film. It was a courageous performance."

Indeed, *Some Like It Hot* became one of Monroe's most successful films, both commercially and critically. Called "the best comedy of the year" by *Time* magazine, it was nominated for five Academy Awards. And though Monroe was not nominated for an Oscar, she did win the Golden Globe Award for Best Actress. Her talent for comedy was celebrated in the reviews, though a comment in the *New York Post* is revealing: "Marilyn does herself proud, giving a performance of such intrinsic quality that you begin to believe she's only being herself." Even after all the changes that Monroe had instigated in her career, the press and public could not distinguish between her real self and her screen persona.

After completing *Some Like It Hot,* she returned to New York to prepare for having her baby. Her longtime gynecologist, Leon Krohn, expressed concern about her physical health and her ability to carry the pregnancy to term. About a month later, his fears came true: Monroe, who had a history of gynecological problems, miscarried. Though she felt defeated in her attempts to have children, she soon fell back into the rhythm of her life in New York. She spent time with her husband and his parents, took acting lessons with Strasberg, visited friends, and discussed movie plans with various producers. She and Miller made arrangements for producing *The Misfits,* the screenplay he was writing for Monroe, and asked the celebrated John Huston to direct it.

Early in 1960, she returned to Hollywood to make *Let's Make Love* for Twentieth Century–Fox. In this comedy, directed by George Cukor, a millionaire pretending to be a poor actor falls in love with a theater actress. Monroe played the actress and French singer Yves

In January 1960, Monroe rehearses her dance moves with choreographer Jack Cole before the filming of *Let's Make Love.* Because dancing on camera made Monroe more nervous than anything else in a movie, Cole was brought in to help her. Cole had also taught Monroe her song-and-dance routines in *Gentlemen Prefer Blondes* and *There's No Business Like Show Business.*

Montand played the millionaire. The rumors circulated that the two stars, who were both married, took the title of the movie literally and had an affair.

Let's Make Love received mixed reviews and is not one of Monroe's noteworthy movies. Nevertheless, Monroe, who was often filled with anxiety during the filming, delivered a strong performance, including four song-and-dance routines. By the end of the production, however, Monroe decided to confront her anxieties and, with the approval of her New York psychiatrist, began sessions with Ralph Greenson, a psychiatrist in Los Angeles. Greenson, like Lee Strasberg, was a confident, overbearing man who became a controversial figure because of the degree to which he involved himself in Monroe's life.

Then, in July 1960, Monroe went on location to Reno, Nevada, to begin shooting *The Misfits*. From the outside, the project seemed ideal. The screenplay was written

Monroe and Yves Montand (center), who costarred in *Let's Make Love*, are shown here at a cocktail party in 1960. Although they both had spouses at the time, rumors circulated that they took the title of their film literally.

especially for Monroe by her husband, a celebrated playwright; it was a far cry from the musicals and comedies that had made her famous; and it featured her in a role that would allow her to show her depth as an actress. Monroe looked forward to working again with director Huston, who had cast her in *The Asphalt Jungle* early in her career. She would also be working with her trusted staff, which she called her "family." Her costars were three highly respected actors, Eli Wallach, Montgomery Clift, and Clark Gable. Wallach and Clift were friends of Monroe's, and Gable was a living legend and longtime idol of hers.

But for everyone involved in the production, the experience of filming *The Misfits* was anything but ideal. In some ways the troubles that plagued this film seemed almost inevitable. There had been strife between factions of Monroe's staff, friends, and colleagues since the filming of *The Prince and the Showgirl* in 1956. These conflicts intensified during *The Misfits,* and new conflicts, especially involving director Huston, originated. Huston, who was as famous for his strong personality as for his filmmaking genius, did not take Monroe seriously and treated her with a disrespect that unnerved her. In one scene in the movie he had old pictures of Monroe, in her pinup girl poses, taped to a wall. "Don't look at those," Monroe, as the character Roslyn Tabor, says. "They're nothing . . . a joke." But the joke did not seem very funny to Monroe. Nor did Huston's habit of referring to her as "dear" and "sweetie." Huston, who spent much of his time gambling at the casinos, had a lack of concern for the cast that upset even veteran actor Clark Gable. The desert heat and the physically strenuous scenes brought additional stress to the entire cast and crew. But the most tension came from the conflict between Monroe and Miller, which further divided the production into contingents.

Monroe and Miller were in the awkward situation of having to work together while their marriage was falling apart. For Monroe this was particularly tortuous because Miller had written the role of Roslyn Tabor as a tribute to her and had put many of his thoughts and feelings about Monroe into the character. Several scenes contained lines and action that were taken almost verbatim from Miller's recollection of scenes from his life with Monroe. Though Miller believed he was writing an honest and revelatory view of Monroe—one that would help her shake the dumb blonde image forever—Monroe felt just as imprisoned by his view of her. As Rupert Allan, Monroe's friend and publicist, explained, she "was desperately unhappy at reading lines written by Miller that were so obviously documenting the real-life Marilyn" and especially objected to his view of her as "naked and wounded."

Roslyn, who meets up with three misfit cowboys in Reno after divorcing her husband, is as aimless and helpless as a child. Though the Gable character calls her "the saddest girl I've ever met," he and his friends are attracted to her energy and goodness and believe she can save them from their dead way of living. She has a naive concern for everything living, and is devastated when the cowboys try to kill a bunch of wild horses. Monroe objected to this scene in particular, because, as she later explained, her character appears "too dumb to explain anything, so I have a fit—a screaming, crazy fit. I mean *nuts*. And to think, Arthur did this to me." About the script and her role, which was supposed to be Miller's tribute to Monroe, she felt, "He could have written me anything, and he comes up with this. If that's what he thinks of me, well, then I'm not for him and he's not for me." To make things worse, the script was incomplete as filming began, and Miller continued writing while they were on location. Monroe was often given last-minute

Eli Wallach (second from left), Montgomery Clift (third from left), Monroe, and Clark Gable (far right) enjoy a rare cheerful moment on the set of *The Misfits* during production in 1960. Arthur Miller (standing near the top of ladder) wrote the screenplay and the acclaimed John Huston (crouching behind Monroe) directed. The production was full of strife and Monroe was offended by the role her husband wrote for her. Their marriage fell apart during the filming of the movie.

script changes on the day they were to be filmed, and for much of the filming she did not know which of the misfits her character was going to end up with.

At one point the production came to a complete halt. Monroe flew back to Los Angeles, where she was hospitalized, and this incident has been recounted often as evidence of Monroe's increasing self-destruction and drug addiction. It is certainly true that Monroe was under enormous physical and emotional strain from the pressures of her career in general and *The Misfits* in particular. It is also true that over the past several years she had become increasingly dependent on various pills—mostly barbiturates and some amphetamines—to relieve the stress, help her sleep, and then help her wake up. These drugs aggravated Monroe's intestinal disorders, making her sick and weak for most of the production. Like many stars of Hollywood's studio era, Monroe had access to prescription medications through a variety of doctors, some of whom were on the studio's payroll. It was sometimes part of the job of a studio doctor to provide the contract players with drugs to help them keep up with their grueling work schedules. Often, as in Monroe's case, the various doctors did not always pay attention to the amounts or types of drugs that the stars were getting from their other doctors as well.

But like almost everything in Monroe's life, there is more than one version of the story of the production difficulties on *The Misfits*. Although it has been common to blame her for almost ruining the production, some have put the blame on Huston, who was infamous for his drinking, gambling, and large ego. According to this version, Huston had run the movie into financial trouble by losing thousands of dollars at the gambling casinos. He had to stop filming because he needed to raise more money. And to cover his mistake, he used Monroe as a scapegoat. He told her doctors that he was worried about her mental condition and drug use and he suggested that filming be suspended while they put her in a hospital.

Eventually, *The Misfits* was completed and well received by the press. Monroe's performance in this drama did help confirm her talents as a serious actress, but the film's mystique comes mainly from the personalities and events associated with it. The team of Monroe, Clark Gable, and Montgomery Clift (another star with a reputation for good looks and self-destructive behavior) added a dimension of intrigue to the film. Gable died soon after the film was completed, and *The Misfits* remains of interest today because it was the last movie made by both him and Monroe.

As *The Misfits* project came to an end, so did the marriage between Monroe and Miller. She was profoundly disappointed in Miller for not giving her the respect or understanding that she most desired. In January 1961, she was granted a divorce in Mexico. Monroe remained on good terms with Miller's family, especially his children and his father. She stayed in her Manhattan apartment and resumed her acting lessons with Strasberg, her sessions with her New York psychiatrist, and her social life with friends and colleagues.

In February, Monroe was hospitalized again. This time, however, she was placed in a psychiatric ward. Her New York psychiatrist, Marianne Kris, who soon admitted that she had made a mistake, checked Monroe in without letting her know that it was a psychiatric hospital. Locked in a room, Monroe felt like she "was in some kind of prison for a crime I hadn't committed." She wrote to the Strasbergs, asking them to get her out of the hospital because "I'm sure to end up a nut too if I stay in this nightmare. Please help me. This is the last place I should be." The Strasbergs were unable to help Monroe because they were not related to her and thus had no authority with the hospital. Finally Monroe was allowed to make a phone call, and she reached her second husband, Joe DiMaggio, who immediately flew up from Florida. DiMaggio, though he was not a relative of Monroe's either, was determined to get her released from the hospital. He demanded that Kris release her, and soon Monroe was out. After resting in a regular hospital, Monroe went to Florida to visit DiMaggio, whom she had not seen in more than five years. She severed all ties with Kris and never saw her again.

Later in 1961, Monroe moved back to Los Angeles and began discussions with producers at Twentieth

Century–Fox. She still owed the studio two films from the contract she had signed earlier, and she agreed, somewhat reluctantly, to make a movie called *Something's Got To Give.* The project involved many respected people, including George Cukor, who had directed Monroe in *Let's Make Love,* screenwriter Nunnally Johnson, and comedian Dean Martin, who was to costar. Like Monroe, however, Cukor and others may have agreed to do the film primarily to fulfill contractual obligations, and the project began in an ambience of indifference. The studio contributed to the dubious merits of the project by assigning it a relatively low budget, which gave many people involved the impression that the studio had initiated the project only to use up the actors' contracts. The Twentieth Century–Fox corporation, like many of the former Big Five movie companies, was in financial

In April 1961, Monroe and DiMaggio arrive in New York from Tampa, Florida, where DiMaggio had taken his former wife to recuperate from a nervous breakdown, which she had after completing *The Misfits.* Monroe's New York psychiatrist, Marianne Kris, had mistakenly placed her in a psychiatric ward without telling her beforehand and DiMaggio came to her aid and demanded that Monroe be released from the hospital into his custody.

trouble, and executives, producers, and writers were being hired and fired at an alarming rate. The project was disorganized, and the script—the story of a shipwrecked woman who comes home to find that her husband has remarried—was not finished when the filming began. In a story conference with Johnson, just one of the many writers assigned to the project, Monroe asked him, "Have *you* been trapped into this, too?"

Once filming got underway, the problems multiplied. There were serious tensions between Monroe and director Cukor, with some reports that Cukor treated her cruelly. The constant script revisions caused Monroe stress with each new page that was delivered to her and further undermined her confidence in the project. And then Monroe, who had a habit of arriving late, missed several days of work because of a viral infection.

Long-standing rumors put most of the blame on Monroe for the problems of *Something's Got To Give.* According to these rumors, her behavior, in large part affected by drug use, was erratic and unreasonable. She would show up late or not at all, could not remember her lines, and was rude to everyone on the set. It is true that Monroe was using a variety of drugs and that she sometimes had trouble with her lines on this and other pictures. But, as with many incidents in her life, it is almost impossible to get to the exact nature of the problems on this film because of the amount of rumor and gossip that have surrounded it.

There are many, for example, who believe that the studio was responsible for the problems on the project, and that the executives perpetuated the stories of Monroe's unruly behavior in order to protect themselves. The dismantling of the studio system and the drop in profits were taking their toll on Twentieth Century–Fox. Like most studios, it was undergoing major restructuring. Most of the executives with whom Monroe had dealt throughout her career had been replaced. And many of the new executives had little experience making movies. Their background was in finance, and they had no feelings of loyalty for Monroe, who for many years had been the studio's biggest star.

But there was another reason why the studio did not give high priority to *Something's Got To Give.* Twentieth Century–Fox was producing another film at the same time, and this film had become a multimillion-dollar fiasco. *Cleopatra,* starring Elizabeth Taylor and Richard Burton, has become notorious as one of the biggest financial disasters in the history of Hollywood. Filmed in Europe, the project went through several actors, directors, and producers and almost ruined the studio financially. In comparison with *Cleopatra,* the complications and the budget overruns of *Something's Got To Give* seemed minuscule. But studio executives believed that the spectacle of *Cleopatra* would save the studio, earn millions, and solve their financial problems. Therefore, the executives in power seem to have supported Taylor's film at the expense of Monroe's and might even have used *Something's Got To Give* to deflect attention from their mismanagement of the company.

As filming progressed, Monroe, who had heard rumors that the studio wanted to fire her, felt increasingly ostracized. She was in constant contact with lawyers and advisers, as well as her psychiatrist, Ralph Greenson, whom she had been seeing regularly since she returned to Los Angeles. Greenson, whose behavior toward his patient was highly unorthodox, had become involved in Monroe's personal and professional affairs. According to Rupert Allan, Monroe's publicist, "Greenson had an amazing amount of control over her life." He had installed a housekeeper, Eunice Murray, in Monroe's home, in part to keep an eye on Monroe, and had joined the payroll at Monroe's studio as a consultant on *Some-*

thing's Got To Give. As things started to break down on the production, Greenson was on a trip abroad, and Monroe, physically weakened, emotionally distraught, and worried about her job and career, asked her psychiatrist to return to help. From the beginning, Greenson had stepped well beyond the usual doctor-patient boundaries with Monroe by involving himself in many aspects of her life besides her psychoanalysis and by breaking the confidentiality ethic, encouraging her to call him or his family at any hour. He flew back to Los Angeles almost immediately to meet with Monroe and to negotiate with the abundance of lawyers and advisers on the project.

In May 1962, Monroe flew to New York to sing "Happy Birthday" at President John F. Kennedy's gala. Shortly after she returned to resume filming, the problems on the movie came to a head, and something finally gave on *Something's Got To Give.* The studio executives claimed that Monroe had breached her contract by repeatedly failing to work and had cost the production more than half a million dollars. They fired her in June.

The news of Monroe's dismissal made headlines all over the country. And the press, which had been an integral part of Monroe's career through the years, perpetuated the stories of Monroe's drug use and erratic behavior. As her former husband Arthur Miller once said, "The press with Marilyn was either at her feet or at her throat," and in the stories about her troubles with the studio, it was clear which position it had taken.

Unquestionably the media, which was getting its version of events from the studio publicists, had overreacted. Monroe and Fox executives soon entered negotiations, and by mid-July they had come to an agreement. The script would be reworked, a new director would be hired, and the filming would resume in October. Monroe, who contributed many ideas to the new script, looked forward to finishing the movie.

8 The Myths of Marilyn Monroe

DESPITE THE SUCCESSFUL RENEGOTIATIONS between Monroe and Twentieth Century–Fox, *Something's Got To Give* was never completed. The reason why—Monroe's death—would become the most controversial event of her life story. Very early in the morning on August 5, 1962, policemen were summoned to Monroe's house, in the Brentwood section of Los Angeles, where they found her, dead, in the bedroom. Eunice Murray, Monroe's housekeeper, explained that she had discovered Monroe and called Greenson, who then called his colleague, Hyman Engelberg, who was Monroe's physician. All three were present when the police arrived, and there are suggestions that several other people had already come and gone from the house. After an autopsy, the coroner determined the cause of death to be an overdose of barbiturates, and possibly a suicide. But it has never been proven conclusively that Monroe committed suicide—despite a reopening of the case in 1982—and this has left the door open for a host of speculations on how and why she died.

Monroe's funeral, arranged by former husband Joe DiMaggio, took place on August 8 at Westwood Memorial Park. DiMaggio carefully chose the

---

Even when she was not happy in her personal life, Marilyn Monroe always maintained her composure and presented herself beautifully to the press and public. She is shown here at a press conference.

guest list and invited only 30 of Monroe's closest friends and associates and no stars or reporters. Among those present were Whitey Snyder; Lee and Paula Strasberg; Ralph Greenson and family; Anne and Mary Karger, the mother and sister of Monroe's former vocal coach and friend Fred Karger; and Monroe's half sister, Berniece Baker Miracle, with whom Monroe had remained in contact for many years. It was Lee Strasberg who delivered the eulogy:

> Marilyn Monroe was a legend. In her own lifetime she created a myth of what a poor girl from a deprived background could attain. For the entire world she became a symbol of the eternal feminine. But I have no words to describe the myth and the legend. Nor would she want us to do so. I did not know this Marilyn Monroe. . . . We . . . knew only Marilyn—a warm human being, impulsive and shy, sensitive and in fear of rejection, yet ever avid for life and reaching out for fulfillment. . . . In our memories of her, she remains alive, not only a shadow on a screen, or a glamorous personality.

But the funeral was in no way the end of the story of Marilyn Monroe. Almost immediately, the public, the press, and her fans began questioning the circumstances of her death and positing theories on how and why she died. These theories, which have grown more fantastic over the years, fall into three main groups. For those who view Monroe's last few years as bleak and self-destructive, the suicide theory is the most believable. According to this view, Monroe had been manipulated her whole life by the studio, the press, the public, and a multitude of doctors, lawyers, advisers, and exploitative friends. Under the pressures of her enormous fame, she became lonely, depressed, and addicted to drugs. Some believe that she had recently had disappointing love affairs with President John F. Kennedy and his brother, Attorney General Robert F. Kennedy. Rumors of Monroe's supposed liai-

In July 1962, Peter Lawford and Monroe relax at the Cal-Neva Lodge in Lake Tahoe, California, where Monroe was a weekend guest of the Lawfords'. Some people believe that near the time of her death, Monroe was on a downward spiral, whereas others claim just the opposite. There is some indication, however, that Monroe was drinking alcohol and consuming pills in large amounts at this time.

sons with the Kennedys had been circulating since she first met Robert Kennedy at a dinner party in October 1961. Though she did meet with both the president and his brother on several other occasions, anything else about these relationships is hard to prove. But, as this theory maintains, the affairs, the drugs, the depression, and the exploitation all contributed to a life spinning out of control. Suicide was the final tragedy in the life of the innocent waif who became a victim of her own stardom.

But others believe that Monroe's life was not unraveling, and that she had every reason to live. At age 36, she had reached a point of calm maturity and seemed to be settling down after years of frequent moving. She had recently purchased a modest single-story home in Brentwood, the first house she ever owned, and put an abundance of time into furnishing it. She was also in the middle of planning several film projects in addition to the rescheduled *Something's Got To Give*. And she seemed to

Monroe's Los Angeles psychiatrist, Ralph Greenson, and his wife, Hildi, were two of the few guests invited to attend Monroe's funeral service. Greenson's relationship with Monroe was considered unorthodox because of the extent to which he involved himself in her career and personal life.

be evaluating other areas of her life as well. There is some evidence that she was about to end her relationships with Greenson, Murray, and others she felt were detrimental to her well-being. There is even a suggestion that she was making preparations to remarry Joe DiMaggio, with whom she had been spending much time. (For nearly 20 years after Monroe's death, DiMaggio had flowers delivered weekly to her crypt, as he had promised when she told him of William Powell's vow to do the same for the dying Jean Harlow.) This version of Monroe's final days rejects the suicide supposition and proposes that she accidentally ingested too many pills, thus making the overdose unintentional.

Still others believe that Monroe was murdered. The murder theories sometimes sound like the plots for Hollywood movies and include a host of suspects and accomplices, including the Kennedys, the FBI, the mafia, the studio, the publicists, the doctors, the coroner, the police department, and various celebrities, among them Frank Sinatra and Peter Lawford. One recent theory, proposed by 1993 biographer Donald Spoto, suggests that Monroe might have died from a kind of accidental murder, at the hands of her psychiatrist Ralph Greenson. Greenson (or housekeeper Murray, acting on Greenson's instructions) may have injected Monroe with a sedative that became fatal when it reacted with the other medications she had already taken.

It will never be known for certain how Marilyn Monroe died. And as with many events in her life, her death has become the focus of conjecture, rumor, and gossip. The mystery surrounding her death soon led to speculation about her life. More than 30 years after her death, books, newspaper and magazine articles, and films continue to offer new views of her life and death. The interpretations are often contradictory, making it difficult to get to the truth about Marilyn Monroe. But one lesson to be learned from studying her life story is the necessity of critically examining the various sources of information. As with any subject, it is crucial to question the motivations of the writers and wonder about their reasons for putting forth their particular theories.

One thing is certain about Monroe's death: it secured her place in the mythology of popular culture. Though she was a legend during her lifetime, her death, with its air of mystery and tragedy, transformed her into an icon. She has intrigued the public more than any other star. That enduring fascination has made her into a symbol of many disparate themes: femininity and sexual allure; the American Dream; the innocence and complacency of the 1950s; the glamour of Hollywood movie stars; the manipulation of the movie business and the publicity machinery; and the evils of greed and exploitation. She has been called a goddess, a victim, and a genius. And though she is famous for these and many other qualities, she has also become a symbol of fame itself.

On August 8, 1962, mourners follow the hearse containing the body of 36-year-old Marilyn Monroe. Monroe's final resting place is the Westwood Memorial Park in Westwood, California.

Of course, when someone becomes an icon, she ceases being a person. In his 1987 autobiography, Arthur Miller said, "A movie star of Marilyn's magnitude is obviously no longer human, but what she is instead is hard to define without calling up the supernatural; she is a form of longing in the public's imagination, and in that sense godlike." Far from being made of stone or celluloid, Monroe was a person, with strengths and weaknesses, successes and failures. And she, perhaps better than anyone else, never confused her true self with her image.

Several of her colleagues have noted her way of referring to Marilyn Monroe in the third person, demonstrating the distance she felt from her public image. Susan Strasberg, the daughter of Lee and Paula Strasberg, once described walking down a street in New York City with Monroe. They were strolling along unnoticed when Monroe said, "Hey do you want to see me be her?" According to Strasberg, Monroe then "made some inner adjustment. Almost like if you see a lamp that's got a bulb in it but the lamp is turned off. All she did was turn the lamp on, and suddenly she started to glow. And people started stopping her—'Oh my god, is that—It can't be—It must be—.'"

Though she could have fun playing Marilyn Monroe, she was also acutely aware of the drawbacks of her well-known image. "Marilyn Monroe became a burden . . . an albatross," she once said, referring to the public's expectations of her and the pressures of living up to those demands. As one of the most famous people in the world, she could say with authority that "Fame is fickle," and that "it's not what fulfills you. It warms you a bit, but the warming is temporary." The lessons she learned about fame are all the more sobering because she had spent much of her life striving to reach that kind of success. Like many children, she had idolized movie stars when she was young and dreamed of becoming one. She then spent every year from the age of 20 developing her skills and working toward those goals. Though she enjoyed her work and was grateful for the public's adoration, she sometimes felt that "being a movie actress was never as much fun as dreaming of being one."

The fame that still surrounds Monroe sometimes threatens to overwhelm her many achievements. She dedicated most of her life to developing herself as an artist. She emerged from the studio era and created a unique screen persona and public image. She combined humor and sexuality in ways that tested the limits of American sexual ethics in the 1950s. She then challenged the studio system for more autonomy over her career and her public image.

In 29 movies she demonstrated a great talent as an actress, comedian, and singer. Witty and charming, she awed almost everyone she met with her charisma. Two of her directors, Joshua Logan and Billy Wilder, remember her as one of the most extraordinary talents with whom they worked. Logan called her "pure cinema" and compared her with Charlie Chaplin and Greta Garbo. "Watch her work," he said, "in any film. How rarely she has to use words. How much she does with her eyes, her lips, with slight, almost accidental, gestures."

As recently as 1994, Wilder, who is still asked about Monroe whenever he makes a public appearance, listed the attributes he so appreciated in her. Speaking of her as if she were still alive, he said, "She has that beautiful, beautiful voice, a great sense of rhythm, and she knows how to read funny dialog and make it ten times as funny." Her early death was a terrible tragedy. But her life was filled with accomplishment. It would only add to the tragedy if the fame and legend of Marilyn Monroe eclipsed her real and remarkable qualities and her admirable achievements.

Further Reading ★ ★ ★ ★ ★ ★ ★ ★ ★ ★ ★ ★ ★ ★ ★

Belmont, Georges. *Marilyn Monroe and the Camera Eye*. Boston: Bulfinch Press, 1989.

Bohn, Thomas W., and Richard L. Stromgren. *Light and Shadows: A History of Motion Pictures*. 3rd ed. Mountain View, CA: Mayfield, 1987.

Conway, Michael, and Mark Ricci. *The Films of Marilyn Monroe*. New York: Lyle Stuart, 1964.

Guiles, Fred Lawrence. *Legend: The Life and Death of Marilyn Monroe*. New York: Stein and Day, 1984.

Mast, Gerald. *A Short History of the Movies*. 3rd ed. Indianapolis: Bobbs-Merrill, 1981.

Miracle, Berniece Baker, and Mona Rae Miracle. *My Sister Marilyn*. Chapel Hill, NC: Algonquin Books of Chapel Hill, 1994.

Norman, Barry. *The Story of Hollywood*. New York: Penguin, 1987.

Rollyson, Carl. *Marilyn Monroe: A Life of the Actress*. New York: Da Capo Press, 1993.

Schatz, Thomas. *The Genius of the System: Hollywood Filmmaking in the Studio Era*. New York: Pantheon, 1988.

Solomon, Aubrey. *Twentieth Century–Fox: A Corporate and Financial History*. Metuchen, NJ: Scarecrow Press, 1986.

Spoto, Donald. *Marilyn Monroe: The Biography*. New York: HarperCollins, 1993.

Steinem, Gloria. *Marilyn*. New York: Henry Holt, 1986.

Summers, Anthony. *Goddess: The Secret Lives of Marilyn Monroe*. New York: Macmillan, 1985.

Weatherby, W. J. *Conversations with Marilyn*. New York: Mason/Charter, 1976.

Zolotow, Maurice. *Marilyn Monroe*. Rev. ed. New York: HarperCollins, 1990.

Appendix ★ ★ ★ ★ ★ ★ ★ ★ ★ ★ ★ ★ ★ ★ ★ ★ ★ ★ ★

THE FILMS OF MARILYN MONROE:

Scudda-Hoo! Scudda-Hay!
   Twentieth Century–Fox, 1948
   (directed by Hugh Herbert)

Dangerous Years
   Twentieth Century–Fox, 1948
   (directed by Arthur Pierson)

Ladies of the Chorus
   Columbia, 1948
   (directed by Phil Karlson)

Love Happy
   United Artists, 1950
   (directed by David Miller)

A Ticket to Tomahawk
   Twentieth Century–Fox, 1950
   (directed by Richard Sale)

The Asphalt Jungle
   MGM, 1950
   (directed by John Huston)

All About Eve
   Twentieth Century–Fox, 1950
   (directed by Joseph L. Mankiewicz)

The Fireball
   Twentieth Century–Fox, 1950
   (directed by Tay Garnett)

Right Cross
   MGM, 1950
   (directed by John Sturges)

Home Town Story
   MGM, 1951
   (directed by Arthur Pierson)

As Young as You Feel
   Twentieth Century–Fox, 1951
   (directed by Harmon Jones)

Love Nest
   Twentieth Century–Fox, 1951
   (directed by Joseph Newman)

Let's Make It Legal
   Twentieth Century–Fox, 1951
   (directed by Richard Sale)

Clash by Night
   RKO, 1952
   (directed by Fritz Lang)

We're Not Married
   Twentieth Century–Fox, 1952
   (directed by Edmund Goulding)

Don't Bother To Knock
   Twentieth Century–Fox, 1952
   (directed by Roy Baker)

Monkey Business
   Twentieth Century–Fox, 1952
   (directed by Howard Hawks)

O. Henry's Full House
   Twentieth Century–Fox, 1952
   (directed by Henry Koster)

Niagara
   Twentieth Century–Fox, 1953
   (directed by Henry Hathaway)

Gentlemen Prefer Blondes
   Twentieth Century–Fox, 1953
   (directed by Howard Hawks)

How To Marry a Millionaire
  Twentieth Century–Fox,
  1953
  (directed by Jean Negulesco)

River of No Return
  Twentieth Century–Fox,
  1954
  (directed by Otto Preminger)

*There's No Business Like Show
  Business*
  Twentieth Century–Fox, 1954
  (directed by Walter Lang)

The Seven Year Itch
  Twentieth Century–Fox, 1955
  (directed by Billy Wilder)

Bus Stop
  Marilyn Monroe Productions,
  1956
  (directed by Joshua Logan)

The Prince and the Showgirl
  Marilyn Monroe Productions,
  1957
  (directed by Laurence Olivier)

Some Like It Hot
  Walter Mirisch/United Artists,
  1959
  (directed by Billy Wilder)

Let's Make Love
  Twentieth Century–Fox, 1960
  (directed by George Cukor)

The Misfits
  United Artists/Seven Arts, 1961
  (directed by John Huston)

Something's Got To Give
  Twentieth Century–Fox, started
  in 1962
  (directed by George Cukor)
  Incomplete

Chronology ★ ★ ★ ★ ★ ★ ★ ★ ★ ★ ★ ★ ★ ★ ★ ★ ★

1926	Born Norma Jeane Mortenson on June 1 in Los Angeles; two weeks later her mother brings her to live with foster family
1933	Returns to live with her mother in Hollywood
1934	Mother hospitalized due to mental illness
1935–42	Norma Jeane lives with foster families, relatives, family friends, and at an orphanage
1942	Quits high school in the middle of her sophomore year and marries Jim Dougherty on June 19
1944	Is discovered by a U.S. Army photographer taking publicity pictures of women working at the Radioplane Company
1945	Signs up with Blue Book Model Agency
1946	Divorces Jim Dougherty; has screen test with Twentieth Century–Fox studio and signs six-month contract; changes name to Marilyn Monroe
1947	Appears in first movie, *Scudda-Hoo! Scudda-Hay!*; begins classes at the Actors Laboratory
1948	Signs six-month contract with Columbia Pictures; begins work with acting coach Natasha Lytess; appears in first major role in the musical *Ladies of the Chorus*; meets agent Johnny Hyde
1949	Poses nude for calendar pictures that become famous three years later
1950	Appears in first reputable film, *The Asphalt Jungle,* directed by John Huston
1951	Signs seven-year contract with Twentieth Century–Fox
1953	Stars in *Niagara*; co-stars in *Gentlemen Prefer Blondes* with Jane Russell; puts handprints and footprints in sidewalk of Grauman's Chinese Theater, a Hollywood landmark

<table>
<tr><td>1954</td><td>Negotiates contract with Twentieth Century–Fox for higher salary and more serious roles after being suspended from the studio on January 4; marries Joe DiMaggio, former New York Yankees baseball player, on January 14; performs for U.S. Army troops stationed in Korea; divorces Joe DiMaggio on October 26</td></tr>
<tr><td>1955</td><td>Stars in The Seven Year Itch, directed by Billy Wilder; moves to New York; forms Marilyn Monroe Productions with Milton Greene; goes on strike from Twentieth Century–Fox; begins studying with Lee Strasberg and the Actors Studio in New York City; begins seeing a psychiatrist on Strasberg's suggestion</td></tr>
<tr><td>1956</td><td>Stars in Bus Stop, directed by Joshua Logan; marries Arthur Miller, Pulitzer Prize–winning playwright, on June 29 and stands by her husband when he is questioned by HUAC; travels to England to film The Prince and the Showgirl with Sir Laurence Olivier and wins the David di Donatello Prize and the Crystal Star Award (the Italian and French equivalents of Academy Awards) for Best Actress</td></tr>
<tr><td>1957</td><td>Miscarries her baby; takes a break from acting</td></tr>
<tr><td>1959</td><td>Stars in Some Like It Hot, directed by Billy Wilder, and goes on to win a Golden Globe Award for her performance; becomes pregnant and miscarries again</td></tr>
<tr><td>1960</td><td>Goes on location to Reno, Nevada, for the filming of The Misfits, written by Arthur Miller</td></tr>
<tr><td>1961</td><td>Divorces Arthur Miller in January; moves back to Los Angeles; agrees to star in Something's Got To Give, a production disaster from which she is fired</td></tr>
<tr><td>1962</td><td>Sings at President John F. Kennedy's birthday gala in New York in May; dies mysteriously in Los Angeles on August 5 at the age of 36</td></tr>
</table>

Index ★

Frances Lefkowitz is a writer and filmmaker. Her short stories have appeared in *Fiction, The Pikestaff Forum,* and the *Northeast Journal,* among other periodicals. She has received a fellowship in literature and an artist project grant in filmmaking, both from the Rhode Island State Council on the Arts. Born and raised in San Francisco, she received a B.A. in anthropology from Brown University and now lives in New York City.

Leeza Gibbons is a reporter for and cohost of the nationally syndicated television program "Entertainment Tonight" and NBC's daily talk show "Leeza." A graduate of the University of South Carolina's School of Journalism, Gibbons joined the on-air staff of "Entertainment Tonight" in 1984 after cohosting WCBS-TV's "Two on the Town" in New York City. Prior to that, she cohosted "PM Magazine" on WFAA-TV in Dallas, Texas, and on KFDM-TV in Beaumont, Texas. Gibbons also hosts the annual "Miss Universe," "Miss U.S.A.," and "Miss Teen U.S.A." pageants, as well as the annual Hollywood Christmas Parade. She is active in a number of charities and has served as the national chairperson for the Spinal Muscular Atrophy Division of the Muscular Dystrophy Association; each September, Gibbons cohosts the National MDA Telethon with Jerry Lewis.